Advance praise for
Smart Selling on the Phone and Online

"*Smart Selling on the Phone and Online* is a comprehensive guide for any sales executive who needs to penetrate the corporate fortress to find and engage prospects in a way that creates value with every connection."

—Gerhard Gschwandtner, Founder and Publisher, *Selling Power*

"*Smart Selling* serves up that all-too-rare combination of insight, experience, relevance, and clarity–all rolled up into a treasure trove of sales tactics that really work."

—Dave Stein, Founder and CEO, ES Research Group, Inc.

"Being strategic has never been so critical, and being smart is necessary. This is a timely book. Josiane Feigon understands what skills are required when selling in today's competitive and uncertain business landscape."

—Mike Smerklo, Chairman and CEO, ServiceSource

"Feigon proves that she knows inside sales inside and out. In *Smart Selling,* she provides a tool kit for inside sales in today's Sales 2.0 world and correctly asserts that timing is integral to success. Feigon offers new tips and tools for 'cubicle warriors' to powerfully connect with time-stressed and increasingly hard-to-catch decision makers, culminating in more opportunities and quicker decisions."

—David Thompson, Co-Founder and CEO, Genius.com;
Founder of Sales 2.0 Conference

"Josiane's book is a comprehensive 'bible' for anyone who wants to sell in the new (Sales 2.0) world."

—Garth Moulton, Co-Founder, *Jigsaw*

"Like you, I've read most of the books about selling out there . . . and Josiane Feigon's is like a breath of fresh spring air! I love both her ideas and the way she presents them. Hers is one of the *very* few books I'd recommend to any sales professional or even my CEO clients."

—Aaron Ross, CEO, PebbleStorm

"Josiane has always shown a tremendous understanding of the sales process, and I consider her a thought leader in evolving sales methodologies to modern times. Effective use of the Internet and the telephone are crucial to keeping cost of sales low, sales executive productivity high, and to staying close to your customers. Any sales or company leader that needs an efficient and effective sales team should read this book."

—Gary Read, President and CEO, Nimsoft

SMART SELLING

on the
Phone and Online

Inside Sales That Gets Results

JOSIANE CHRIQUI FEIGON

AMACOM

American Management Association

New York • Atlanta • Brussels • Chicago • Mexico City • San Francisco
Shanghai • Tokyo • Toronto • Washington, D.C.

This publication is designed to provide accurate and authoritative
information in regard to the subject matter covered. It is sold with the
understanding that the publisher is not engaged in rendering legal,
accounting, or other professional service. If legal advice or other expert
assistance is required, the services of a competent professional person should
be sought.

Library of Congress Cataloging-in-Publication Data

Feigon, Josiane Chriqui.
    Smart selling on the phone and online : inside sales that gets results
/ Josiane Chriqui Feigon.
        p.   cm.
    Includes index.
    ISBN-13: 978-0-8144-1465-1
    ISBN-10: 0-8144-1465-6
    1. Telephone selling.   2. Electronic commerce.   3. Selling.
I. Title.
    HF5438.3.F436   2010
    658.8′72—dc22

                                            2009012583

Printing number

10   9   8   7

For my mother, Juliette Chriqui,
who always believed I had something important to say

CONTENTS

FOREWORD

When I first began my sales career at Xerox, we were expected to make 30–50 cold calls per week. Each day I'd jump in my car and head out to my territory to prospect for new customers. And as a Minnesota resident, I really know what cold-calling means. Even blizzard conditions with −20 degree temperatures never interfered with my prospecting. Knocking on doors was how you got business. If you couldn't meet eyeball-to-eyeball, you weren't selling.

Fast-forward 25 years and the sales landscape has radically changed. Stressed out, overworked corporate decision makers view time as their most precious commodity. The last thing they want is to have a self-serving salesperson sitting across from them, babbling incessantly about their leading-edge solution or unique methodology.

So, they erect a virtually impenetrable barricade around themselves. They refuse to meet with cold callers. Plus, they rarely answer the phone, roll all calls to voicemail, and seldom return messages. The average seller finds it extremely difficult to connect with decision makers, deliver compelling messages, and set up appointments without getting brushed off.

I know this from personal experience! During the dotcom bust, my own business collapsed and I had to rebuild it from scratch. Once I figured out what it took to crack into corporate accounts in today's business environment, I wrote *Selling to Big Companies* for outside salespeople and entrepreneurs who were pursuing opportunities with these larger firms.

It became readily apparent to me that selling both on the phone and online requires a specialized skill set that doesn't come naturally to many salespeople. Here's what I saw them struggle with:

> Capturing the attention of corporate decision makers due to the lack of customer-enticing messaging.

> Getting stuck with the wrong decision makers and staying there, enabling competitors to get a toehold in the account.

> Establishing trust and building relationships with people when they couldn't meet in person.

> Poor sales productivity because they didn't know how to effectively leverage available technology, without getting sucked into it.

> Managing a large database of prospects, numerous concurrent opportunities, and all the associated tasks required to advance the sales process.

> Nurturing and re-engaging prospective customers to ensure they're top of mind when it's decision time.

> Not getting in the "flow" that's needed to be at the top of their game due to sporadic prospecting.

As you can see, the challenges are big for anyone who sells on the phone and online. But in the past decade, there's been an explosion of companies who have set up dedicated inside sales teams to augment or even replace their direct sales force. These inside salespeople deal with these issues all day and every day, thus further magnifying the challenge.

To be successful, inside salespeople need different skills that are distinct and relevant for their profession. And I can't think of a better person to teach them than Josiane Feigon, President of Telesmart Communications. Her customized sales training programs for inbound and outbound inside sales teams teach people how to "think and talk on the phone at the same time." While that last statement may make you smile, if you've ever frozen up while talking to a prospect like I have, you know why it's so important!

I first discovered Josiane's TeleSmart blog three years ago and was immediately impressed with her obvious expertise in working with inside sales teams. She was one of the early sales bloggers and wrote with a refreshing, candid style. Her strategies and techniques were 100% congruent with what I'd found was essential for sales success, but tailored for the needs of the inside salesperson.

It's not often I find someone who challenges my own thinking, but that's what I get from Josiane. I love her fresh perspectives on how to proactively go after targeted accounts, keep the pipeline full, and maintain momentum. I value her kick-butt advice on how to gain control over the everyday chaos and competing priorities. I appreciate her practical tips and step-by-step guidance on how to engage prospects, create value, and close the sale. And, in her inimitable style, Josiane deftly leads you through what it takes to be a savvy and successful inside salesperson. It's just like having a good friend at your side!

Inside sales has come a long way since the "Telephonics" workshop I attended over 20 years ago—when selling over the phone was still new and the Internet had yet to be born. In *Rethinking the Sales Force* (McGraw-Hill, 1999), Neil Rackham and John DeVincentis wrote about the emergence of sales specialties such as appointment setting and proposal writing. But I don't think they could ever have imagined just how important, productive, and profitable inside sales would become in the past decade.

If your company has an inside sales organization that's primarily doing customer service, it's time to upgrade their skills. If your expensive field sales team is wondering how they can be successful with reduced travel and entertainment expenses, this book is for them.

Wishing you great sales success.

Jill Konrath
Author, *Selling to Big Companies*

ACKNOWLEDGMENTS

My deepest gratitude goes to Naomi Lucks for finding my real voice buried somewhere underneath the rubble and bringing it back to me on a platter, and to Bob Nirkind at AMACOM who knew he would publish my book before I ever knew.

My heartfelt thanks to Gwen Wagner—my muse, collaborator, and the most talented instructional designer I've ever met. To Martha Holmes for her brilliant and intelligent feedback throughout the years. For my early mentors who taught me so much about sales, Bryan Wilson, and training and communication, Sharon Marks.

The inside sales space is a crazy place to hang out, so thanks to my PhoneWorks partners, Sally Duby and Anneke Sealy, for making it fun and bringing life to it. In writing this book, I had a group of enthusiastic supporters—my advice council—who were always there for me with their infinite wisdom, insight, and great suggestions. Thanks to Janet Boss, Andy Creach, Elaine Chan, Chris Rollings, Mitch Stewart, Tracy Walton, Sherman Hu, Benjamin Nachbaur, Pablo Pollard, and Shelly Davenport.

I have been so lucky to have the best clients on the planet; they have put their trust in me and supported all my projects. My work would never have been possible without my inside sales warriors, managers, and all training participants who showed up, listened, learned, read my blog, followed me on Twitter, and remembered to try a new skill or idea. I promise to always stay fresh, current, and never get stale on you guys.

For my family—especially my sisters, Colette Grey and Sandi Bouhadana, who are my lifelines. And for my father, Sidney Chriqui, who taught me to appreciate the written and spoken word. And for all my awesome friends and extended family who may now have a better understanding of what I do after reading this book. Last but not least, for my daughter Briana, who lights up my heart and gives me purpose.

INTRODUCTION
But I've Only Got Four Minutes!

You've just returned from your sales kickoff meeting, inundated with products, tools, systems, and technical information on your company. You got to party with your field partners, and agreed that you guys would kill your numbers this year. It was exciting to see the inside teams get acknowledged for all their work last year—but with that acknowledgment came a new, higher quota from your manager. So here you are, back in your cubicle, with a laptop, high-resolution monitor, whiteboard, your Blackberry, and a phone. You are pumped, psyched, and ready to get out there, but—no one is answering their phones or responding to your e-mails, and your pipeline is looking pretty bare. When you do manage to connect, all you hear is, "No thanks, we're set . . ." or "Call me at the beginning of next quarter." And even though you think you only have about four minutes to spare, you decide to open up this book.

Congratulations! You've already taken your first step to becoming a smart-selling inside sales pro ready to be transformed into a savvy Sales 2.0 warrior who is ready to take on today's opt-out busy crowd. Reading this book will help you survive and thrive through your sales messaging: You'll learn how to craft introductions that get prospects talking, how to get out of the No-Po zone and align with power buyers, how to make presentations that have real selling power, how to field objections and turn them into opportunities, and how to build a healthy—and accurate!—sales forecast.

FINALLY! A BOOK WRITTEN JUST FOR YOU

Whether you are in inside sales, telesales, lead development, lead generation, lead qualification, renewals, or are basically spending fifty-plus hours a week calling on distracted, risk-averse business professionals who only give you four minutes of their time, this book is written for you.

If you are one of those time-crunched managers meeting with your inside team each week wondering what's holding them back from hitting their numbers, this book is for you.

If you have an inside organization contributing to your sales numbers or qualifying leads for you, and you're wondering how they can get some skills training fast, this book is for you.

And if you find yourself wondering what the plastic golf sets and huge trophies filled with candy are doing in some people's cubicles, and why other sales reps' names are on the "wall of shame," this book is for you.

This robust and comprehensive ten-step sales system includes ten essential skills inside sales warriors must have in order to effectively sell by phone and online in today's Sales 2.0 world. Inside salespeople are riding the crest of the wave of change in the way sales are made. This book gives you the robust skills you need to master this sales transformation right now.

SELLING IN A SALES 2.0 WORLD

Less than a decade ago, customers expected to receive an in-person visit from their field sales rep. Today, veteran field reps are scrambling to keep up with the new B2B stars. Inside salespeople, once the "neglected stepchildren" of sales organizations, have changed the way sales are done. Businesses now rely on inside sales teams to generate up to 50 percent of their revenue. Inside salespeople prospect and manage customers at the highest levels: cold-calling directors, VPs, and C-level decision makers within some of the largest companies in the world. They are bright, educated, culturally diverse, sophisticated, and extremely well-paid professionals who sell complex solutions worth millions of dollars over the phone and online.

Today's market, economic, and competitive conditions have created a more complex and less predictable sales cycle. And that means more of everything. As companies provide more tools, technologies, and systems to help speed up the sales cycle and increase efficiency and productivity, only sales reps who can seamlessly integrate the necessary tools, technologies, and systems into their sales process can earn the right to be called inside sales warriors.

Think about it: Inside salespeople average *two hundred* new outbound calls and e-mails per week, risking rejection on an hourly basis. As a salesperson alone with your phone in a warren of cubicles, you may feel isolated and unmotivated. This book is your true friend and companion as it sits inside your cubicle with you and helps you make some simple changes—such as crafting a new opening statement, creating an original e-mail template, or generating fresh questions—that transform hang-ups and rejections into new prospects and closed deals.

WHY I WROTE THIS BOOK

I know inside sales from the inside out—literally, from inside the cubicle to the mind of the customer. And I understand inside sales warriors well enough to know that they are tired of training sessions geared for field reps and books that just don't get it. They are annoyed when people misunderstand them and believe they are "smile and dial" phone jocks who just "churn and burn" through calls. This book reflects the whole spectrum of my work: as a trainer who knows the skills inside sales reps need; as a coach who knows how to get up close and personal to figure out where the rep is going wrong and how to set it right; as a consultant who has performed many inside sales audits; as a thought leader who predicts trends and forecasts in the industry; as an advocate for inside sales who believes they are the most talented sales group; and as a former inside sales rep and an entrepreneur who has single-handedly grown her own organization by walking her talk.

For fifteen-plus years I've owned TeleSmart Communications, a San Francisco–based global training organization specializing in inside sales training, coaching, and consulting. Our TeleSmart 10 program is the ten-step skills program that continues to be chosen as the flagship methodology for global fast-growing inside sales organizations. For more than twenty-five years, I've carved a niche with some of the most talented and progressive Fortune 1000 high-tech companies in the world. I have certified 10,000-plus teams and managers on TeleSmart methodology.

I have also spent 5,000-plus hours listening to calls with a training Y and observing inside sales reps on the job, hearing both sides of the conversation. I know your side—how you work, your self-talk, what motivates you, what you are fearful of, and how you can unknowingly sabotage your success. And I know your customers' or prospects' side—the people who are sitting at their desks reading e-mail, looking at their caller ID, and not picking up the phone when they see a vendor calling. I also know how the Sales 2.0 landscape has changed everything, including the old selling rules.

This book is not homework: I know you don't have extra time! It's designed to be read and digested on the job—your daily drip of tactical skills and solutions that you can test out immediately. I know you are impatient and will want to speed through it—or maybe just go straight to Chapter 9, "Closing"—but I encourage you to read it from beginning to end. Why? Because each skill builds on the one before it exponentially, resulting in big changes. Each chapter is packed with tons of useful tips, fresh ideas, trend info, and insights into why you do what you do and why your customers do what they do. It also includes both phone and e-mail tips, as these are the dynamic duo for inside sales warriors today.

So shut off your IM buddy list, stop texting for a few minutes, turn off your e-mail, find the nearest conference room that you won't get kicked out of for a few hours, and go hang out with this book.

Welcome to the inside sales warrior club! You have arrived!

A BRIEF TOUR OF THIS BOOK

Smart Selling from the Inside Out is a complete training guide to the TeleSmart 10 System for Power Selling: the essential skills you'll need for success. Each chapter is information-rich, and each skill is a way to generate more income. This book gives you the big picture, taking you inside the sales cycle—because these skills are designed to work with the *entire* sales cycle, not just a part of it. It also takes you inside the workings of the brave new Sales 2.0 world that has changed the way sales are done.

Take a moment to open up the dessert menu. Review every delicious chapter—each one is specifically designed to make you money and make you a stronger salesperson.

Chapter 1—Time Management: Momentum Control

Your organization understands the value inside sales brings, and they want you to have all the perks. So they throw a glut of web-based tools at you and tell you to go be productive. But the truth is that you are drowning in this data, overwhelmed with learning new tools, searching for other tools, and paralyzed by these disparate systems. You'd love to recapture your time and work proactively for new business opportunities, but you're constantly distracted and pulled in a million directions. That's where time management comes in—right at the beginning. In this chapter you will learn:

- ⊘ To make a map of your sales process by creating a daily activity plan to work with your territory plan
- ⊘ To maintain self-discipline in blocking a few hours per day for your non-negotiable power calls
- ⊘ To create a clear call objective prior to making each call
- ⊘ To say "no," shut off distractions, and learn to work smarter and faster
- ⊘ To save time and maintain your focus in seven steps

Chapter 2—Introducing: Selling in Sound Bites

Have you been losing calls lately, wondering if the battery is out on your headset or your cell phone? Or maybe it's just you? It's not you.

It's that you're selling in a noisy, crowded, fast-paced market, calling distracted, risk-averse, busy decision makers who have short attention spans. They also have low tolerance for vendors, and often choose to opt out of sales introductions. But cold-calling and voice mail are not dead! They are very much alive, and so is your message. How can you make yourself stand out in their overloaded inboxes and heavily screened phone systems? In this chapter you will learn:

- To understand how Sales 2.0 trends are impacting messaging etiquette
- To combine e-mail and voice mail messaging for a dynamic one-two introduction
- The important components in e-mail messaging
- How to stay ahead of trends in e-mail
- To identify strong opening probes that initiate a call and invite the prospect to talk
- The multiple touch rule and how to use it

Chapter 3—Navigating: Avoiding the No-Po's

Have you lost sales because you realized—too late—that you were hanging out with a powerless decision maker? You were sure they were going to buy—they had a fancy title, they understood and loved your solution, they kept promising they would buy only after they saw one more competitive analysis, and they even had you redesign the proposal. But when it came time to pull the trigger, it was obvious you were talking with a No-Po—someone with no power, no potential, and no purchase order. This quick lesson on power—how it hides, moves, and becomes invisible—loads you up with support and reinforcement. In this chapter you'll learn:

- Why we love our No-Po's and why we keep hanging on
- The ten flags that identify No-Po's, and how to avoid them
- To build an org chart that helps you find the power
- To discern whether particular gatekeepers can help or hurt the sales process

⊘ To understand the underlying political structures that influence the decision-making process in any organization

Chapter 4—Questioning: Building Trust, One Question at a Time

Do you find yourself hanging up from a call wondering why you forgot to ask certain basic questions? When access is granted and you only have seconds, what questions do you ask to quickly engage and earn more time? Strong questioning skills can help you capture control of the call and lead a sale to close. These are vital skills! Today's prospects have lost patience with vendor questions—they are tired of the same questions, and annoyed with outdated sales tactics. We'll explore the art of questioning in depth, teaching you to use your questions to gain important information painlessly, to probe deeper to uncover hidden needs, and to guide the prospect through the call with a strong plan. In this chapter you'll learn:

⊘ To understand the order, strategy, style, formulation, and criteria of effective questioning
⊘ To differentiate between telling and selling
⊘ To organize your questions using established qualification criteria
⊘ To gain analytical questioning skills
⊘ To focus on formulating questions that get the answers you need

Chapter 5—Listening: Letting Go of Assumptions

If you really listen to your prospects, this is what you'll hear: they're tired of salespeople telling them what they need, and angry at being misunderstood by quota-pressured reps that could care less about them and just need to set appointments or close a deal. And they also need a vendor like you to make their pain go away! It is only by actively listening that you will discover what their pain is, and whether or not they are No-Po's. But that doesn't mean hearing what you want to believe, or simply waiting for your turn to talk. It means actively listening and diving deeper into your questioning efforts. This chapter takes an active and aggressive approach to listening, encouraging salespeople to think intuitively, listen strategically for new opportunities, and document, document, document! In this chapter you'll learn:

- ⊘ How to use data integrity, and to integrate online and offline note-taking and documentation techniques into your needs discovery strategy
- ⊘ To develop effective pain/impact questioning skills
- ⊘ To actively listen through precision questioning and paraphrasing
- ⊘ How to gain the confidence of difficult telephone personalities

Chapter 6—Linking: Selling to Power Buyers

Are you ready to talk with a power buyer? Or have you spent so much of your time talking with a No-Po that you would inadvertently sabotage your success if you did connect with a power buyer? These busy executives can be unforgiving if they're not approached in the right way. Reps who fail to capture their attention are shown the virtual door pretty quickly. But how do you find them, what do they want to hear, and how do you say it so they hear it? In this chapter you'll learn:

- ⊘ How to align with influence
- ⊘ How to recognize power buyers over the phone and on e-mail
- ⊘ How to get comfortable with the altitude at C-level
- ⊘ How to tune into the "alpha" influencer, the executive assistant
- ⊘ How to keep finding power as it jumps around the org chart
- ⊘ How to adjust your language and message to different titles within the corporate hierarchy
- ⊘ Daily affirmations to boost your confidence and self-esteem

Chapter 7—Presenting: It's Showtime!

Today's time-stressed decision makers don't take the time to read the attachments you send them or sit through long webinars. Yet the numbers of people using web conferencing is increasing exponentially. Making web presentations is becoming the most essential part of the sales cycle, although many quickly devolve into "death by PowerPoint." This chapter explores various presentation vehicles and teaches the essentials of web/video conferencing and other online tools. It guides you through the ins and outs of executing and pitching perfectly, whether you get a five-minute phone meeting or a thirty-minute web conference. In this chapter, you'll learn:

> How to design and deliver effective online, web, and video demos and presentations
> How to select PowerPoint slides that help you sell
> How to succinctly educate, motivate, and influence others on your product or service
> How to ask closing questions that move the presentation along
> How to articulate the competitive advantages of your product/service

Chapter 8—Handling Objections: Bring Them On!

Do you feel like you're being swamped by a tidal wave of objections? They come in the same flavors they always have, but now they're delivered via e-mail, text, phone, and chat. However you get them, objections are never easy. But when you can be ready for them, with responses that make sense to prospects, you can say, "Bring it on!" This chapter explores fears that can actually create objections, and how to break through your own resistance. You'll learn to identify five major categories of customer objections, and learn how to effectively rebound, gain confidence, and overcome them. Finally, you'll take away the Comeback Pack—a set of rebuttal questions, phrases, and comebacks to use every time. In this chapter you'll learn:

⊘ To understand the barriers you create and how resistance keeps you down
⊘ Common reasons that customers resist
⊘ To differentiate between spoken and silent objections
⊘ To recognize warning signs that your sales may be in danger

- ⊘ Why your prospect sometimes goes radio silent on you
- ⊘ To decipher e-mail objections and how to rebut them
- ⊘ To arm yourself with the Comeback Pack—one hundred rebuttal solutions you can use right now

Chapter 9—Closing: The Complex Road to Gaining Commitment

Closing is where the rubber meets the road. It's about using all of your skills, believing you really deserve the business, and refusing to accept the possibility of losing the sale to your competitor. It's also about building and managing a healthy sales funnel that doesn't have you resorting to desperate discounting measures at the end of the month just to bring your numbers in. In this chapter you'll learn:

- ⊘ How to analyze your sales funnel: build a high-quality, smoothly running funnel every month
- ⊘ To ask the most appropriate questions at each stage of the sales process, and especially when you hear closing signals
- ⊘ How to create momentum via compelling events throughout the sales cycle
- ⊘ To make sure you get a daily dose of self-confidence
- ⊘ Valuable end-of-quarter motivational success stories from sales reps

Chapter 10—Partnering: Conscious Collaboration

I know, you haven't been happy with your field partner lately. In the past, customers wanted more feet on the street. Today, they want more knowledge online and by phone. That's why inside sales is part of a larger integrated team of sales specialists all supporting the customer. The trick is to remember that you are not at the mercy of your stressed-out, disorganized partner. You can be proactive and put yourself in the driver's seat, partnering with your field rep, creating strategic alliances outside the company, and socially networking your way to bigger and better things. In this chapter you'll learn:

- ☑ How to articulate the value of a team-selling approach
- ☑ How to build your virtual team
- ☑ How to determine your partner readiness criteria
- ☑ To quantify the trust factor you bring to a partnership
- ☑ To identify strong and weak partnerships
- ☑ To design contracts and agreements for strong partnering

BE A CUBICLE WARRIOR!

What's this book doing in your cubicle? It's there to help you sell.

I really do want you to finish this book and learn *all* the skills you'll ever need. Keep it around, refer to it when you need to, and use it to help you do what you do best *even better.*

Ready?

Let's get this party started!

CHAPTER 1

TIME MANAGEMENT

Momentum Control

Your time is limited, so don't waste
it living someone else's life.

—Steve Jobs

In this chapter, you'll get valuable insight into:

- ⊘ The effects of having less time control
- ⊘ Sales 2.0 overload for the sales rep
- ⊘ When paralysis sets in
- ⊘ Living in reactive mode

You'll learn tools and tactics to help you:

- ⊘ Regain your momentum and recapture time and take control
- ⊘ Understand how to differentiate between reactive and proactive
- ⊘ Say "no" and shut off distractions and learn to work smarter and faster
- ⊘ Learn the importance of creating a daily activity plan to work with your territory plan
- ⊘ Maintain self-discipline in blocking a few hours per day for your non-negotiable power calls
- ⊘ Create a clear call objective prior to making each call

Susan isn't ready for our scheduled coaching session—a web conference is running overtime. "I'll just be a few more minutes," she whispers, waving me into her cubicle and pointing at a chair.

While on her web conference, she receives an instant message from her manager. He requests that all deals be entered into Salesforce.com (SFA) before end of day if she expects to get credit for them. He also wants her forecast report. Meanwhile, her cell phone vibrates and she reads a text message sent by her UK partner: "The deal is ours for $80K this month & not $120K." She groans. That means she's going to have to revise the proposal to include the new terms and get it out to him before the end of his day—hours away from her time zone.

Suddenly, she slams her hand on her desk. "Don't tell me this is happening again!" Susan's system has locked up—a regular occurrence, apparently. Her company merged with a competitor a few months ago, and the systems haven't been integrated or upgraded. Data is not efficiently shared or retrieved, which means too many windows and programs open all at once, which inevitably makes the systems crash. Susan looks at me with her last shred of optimism. "Just give me a few extra minutes to check my voice mail!"

She finds eight new voice mail messages—all marked urgent and requiring immediate attention—along with several dozen e-mails from her customers, external partners, internal departments, and several regional managers. Susan looks at her watch and glances at a series of clocks all neatly aligned on her desk. It's noon now in California, 2:00 p.m. in Austin, 3:00 p.m. in Atlanta, and 9:00 p.m. in the UK and Latin America.

"There goes my morning again," she says, shaking her head. "Ever since I walked in, I've been putting out fires!" Her field partner pops his head into her cubicle to ask if they can spend time strategizing on their target list before he leaves for the airport, and she agrees to meet with him after our coaching session. Just as he leaves, she receives an instant message from her regional manager, who wants her to attend the all-hands meeting in the afternoon because the worldwide VP will be making an announcement on new fiscal initiatives that address her new compensation. After attending this meeting, it looks like she's expected to sit in on a meeting with the marketing organization to discuss lead quality and conversion. They're planning a marketing blast campaign this week to over 300,000 prospects and they need input from the team on their target audience. Susan gives me a panicked look.

"I think we need to reschedule our coaching session for another time," I suggest.

INSIDE SALES IS ABOUT *TIME*

Yes, inside sales is about money. But perhaps more important, it's about *time:* how you plan it, and how you use it to your best advantage. There is a direct correlation between time control and quota attainment. The choices you make, the focus you keep, the plan you produce, the way you organize your e-mail, the order in which you ask questions, and the momentum you create and maintain set the foundation for your phone and online sales success.

Less Time to Sell

Precall research averages forty-five minutes for just one contact. It takes from five to seven attempts to reach your contact by phone or e-mail before they actually respond. You have to make enough initial calls and follow-up calls to generate genuine prospects you can confidently put in your pipeline. Meanwhile, the phone keeps ringing, texts and e-mails are flooding your inbox, your boss needs your forecast by this afternoon, and you're *already* eating lunch in your cubicle. In the sometimes unpredictable Sales 2.0 world, it's easy to lose time multitasking inefficiently, lose track of time, lose focus, and lose sales in the process. And if your momentum gets tripped up, that leads to procrastination and wrong choices.

Less Control Over How Your Time Is Spent

It's no secret: inside salespeople are more frustrated with their time management and have less control than ever before. The good news is that they are finally receiving the recognition they deserve, as they are now a vital part of the entire sales process. But the bad news is that increased demands, requests, deadlines, and initiatives have been added to their daily responsibilities on a regular basis. That means having less control over how your time is spent.

The days of sitting in neatly lined sales cubicles cold-calling and prospecting sixty calls per day are over. An inside salesperson is not only part of an integrated and virtual team; he or she is the point person who leads, coordinates, facilitates, educates, and runs with the sale. The salesperson's workday starts on a Sunday night to meet the demands of his or her globally disbursed geographical territories and their virtual partners. Salespeople are still driven by metrics that help them build a daily, weekly, and monthly funnel of prospects—which they must "touch" at least nine to twelve times and can forecast to a close. And on top of all this, they must maintain systems, manage complex sales processes, and work with more sales tools than they know what to do with.

Welcome to Sales 2.0 Overload

If you've been around long enough, you remember the good old days: selling with a Rolodex of accounts, prospecting for new ones using the *Business Times,* manually entering orders, tracking the number of calls you make each day on a tick sheet, and using an Excel spreadsheet to forecast your deals. Today, these tools are a thing of the past. The evolution of Web 2.0 has paved the way for the excesses of Sales 2.0. A glut of new web-based tools, technologies, and processes—all designed to help speed up the sales cycle, increase sales efficiencies, and close more opportunities faster—have inundated the market. All these tools and systems *should* be a big help. But in reality, inside salespeople are drowning in data, overwhelmed with learning new tools, searching for other tools, and paralyzed by these disparate systems.

The very nature of inside sales means managing the sales engine from the inside—no travel, no getting outside the box. Inside salespeople are active throughout the sales cycle, and they must also manage the technology, tools, and process *before and after* the sale even happens. Inevitably, they become the "data hounds" of their sales organization.

An average inside salesperson may manage data and metrics from at least two dozen different tools in order to progress their sale. They maintain, track, and enter customer data into at least a half-dozen systems. And—if they could just remember their log-in password!— there are many more licenses that are just waiting to be accessed and used. All these sophisticated tools are designed to track everything from routine contact and account management to, increasingly, opportunity management and prospect collaboration. Most plug in to the central repository that tracks contact information, sales metrics, and performance.

Before making a call, salespeople can choose from dozens of pre-call research and planning tools available to help them search their prospect company and gather names and contacts. During their sales cycle, they can use web conferencing tools to hold online meetings. After a call, their phone system tracks volume and talk time to identify performance and provide trends and analysis at a macro level for model refinement.

Inevitably, the tools designed to help reps sell efficiently lead to *less* productivity.

LESS TIME LEADS TO MORE PARALYSIS

The natural response to daily overload is frustration, the belief that time is beyond your control, and an increasingly desperate scramble to get a handle on your day. Some believe that working faster and multitasking will help get them caught up; some make poor choices because they can't take the time to separate the urgent from the truly important. As they attempt to respond to the overload, paralysis sets in. They can only sit and watch as revenue dollars hemorrhage away.

The toll that interruptions and distractions take on productivity is significant. A study conducted by the University of California in 2008 found the average salesperson is distracted every eleven minutes, and with each distraction it takes them an average of twenty-five minutes to return to their task. These distractions range from the simple desktop "noise" of e-mail, voice mail, and text messaging to trouble with tools and systems. CSO Insights' 2008 Performance Optimization Survey also confirms the time salespeople spent on non-sales activities is increasing. When you add the inevitable external interruptions, there's a constant stream of obstacles coming at them to interrupt their momentum and keep them from rebounding or multitasking efficiently to get back on track with sales calls.

Call Activity Paralysis

Call activity, otherwise known as phone activity, is at an all-time low. Inside salespeople are slowing down on their phone calls primarily because they find they are wasting so much time leaving voice mail messages rather than getting a live person on the phone. Some standard metrics indicate the typical inside salesperson is making an average of just eight to twelve outbound calls per day and their total talk time averages thirty-three minutes a day.

E-Mail Paralysis

E-mail is replacing phone efforts, but even this is a problem because most inside salespeople do not have an efficient marketing and sales strategy in mind before pressing the "send" key. They are spending too much time crafting individualized e-mails for prospects and reinventing new e-mails after each call or writing long e-mails with lots of attachments that never get opened.

Value Messaging Paralysis

Attempting to clearly articulate a value proposition can cause paralysis. When sales reps spend 80 percent of their time leaving meaningless voice mail messages, they don't know what to do if by some miracle they actually get a live person on the call! Call openings, call objectives, and value introductions are sloppy, and their product pitch is confusing, so they don't earn enough time to stay on the call.

Lead Management Paralysis

Inside salespeople are always complaining they lack leads—yet they continue to make wrong choices on the ones they have. They either hold on to bad leads too long or let go of good leads too soon. They lack the patience of cultivating the lead through a series of sales stages—whether it is six-step sales stages or eight-step sales stages. When this process is missing, it affects the lead generation, qualification, and conversion processes, resulting in weak and unclear lead hand-off to the field.

Qualification Paralysis

Reps keep asking prospects the same questions, mainly about budget and timeframe. They're missing a strong qualification process, which leaves them without a way to determine what constitutes a weak or strong lead—especially if they receive a response from a nonqualified decision maker. This leads to time wasted puzzling out who's really a lead and who's not.

Tools Paralysis

The abundance of available sales tools can cause paralysis on its own—and some tools are just good excuses to waste time and hide behind. In a recent survey, salespeople spent an average of forty-five minutes in precall planning researching their prospect company and preparing for the call. Yet when they finally got a live voice—after averaging twenty-one dials—they only got about fourteen seconds on the phone and two seconds on e-mail. The skills required to earn time by delivering a powerful value statement are not there.

Prioritization Paralysis

When so many issues demand attention at the same time, it's difficult to differentiate the urgent from the important. Just getting the fire hose out and putting out fires as you see them is the comfortable and familiar way of attacking pressing issues—but it doesn't work. There are always more issues coming at you. Taking the time to prioritize, and to learn faster and more efficient ways to work productively, will save you time in the long run.

Power Paralysis

Aligning with the wrong decision maker, calling the same contact over and over and expecting different results, and failing to find the power decision maker are some of the biggest time wasters—and very common. At least half of all forecasted opportunities are lost because the salesperson not only aligned with the wrong power source, but felt too paralyzed to go around the source because he or she was too deep in the sales cycle and had too much time already invested in the effort.

Pipeline Paralysis

Building a healthy pipeline is what it's all about, yet many are becoming increasingly impatient and looking for a quick fix to increase their revenues. Most pipeline-building efforts happen toward the end of the month, and it's a scramble to get business closed at the last minute. If salespeople go after "low-hanging fruit," also known as "bluebirds" or "run rate" business, they are not being proactive in building their pipeline. One reason for this is because forecasting is becoming more unpredictable as the sales cycle continues to grow.

Planning Paralysis

Planning is not given a high value in many sales organizations. It trickles down from management to sales as a "non-revenue-generating activity"—that is, not a good use of time. Unfortunately, nothing could be further from the truth.

If the salesperson has a plan, it gets extinguished by upper management's agenda, or, the pressure to hit the number overshadows the importance of planning. And if and when salespeople plan, they don't even know where to begin to plan or what to include in their plan. They clearly don't have the skills to plan correctly, because they have never been given the time! Too many salespeople lack the ability to design a daily activity plan, a weekly account plan, or a quarterly territory plan.

Seven Ways to Save Time and Maintain Your Focus

1. Increase your talk time: the human voice is still your best tool.
2. Call deeper and wider rather than leaving too many voice mail messages for one contact.

3. Learn to quickly identify strong prospects and ask tough questions early in the call.

4. Ask for less time from prospects—follow the under six-minute rule, which means you should only request under six minutes.

5. Hold on to good leads, but let go of unproductive leads you've held onto for too long.

6. Focus on what you *can* control, and let go of issues beyond your control.

7. Be flexible as to when you contact a new prospect—"rules" about "the best time of day" can waste valuable time.

BE PROACTIVE IN A REACTIVE WORLD

In today's fear-driven, high-pressure world, it's easy to become highly reactive—responding equally and frantically to each issue as it happens, without taking the time to distinguish urgent from the important. When we spend all our time being reactive, it's not long before we become frantic. And when we operate in frantic mode all the time, time flies out the window. Fortunately, we can implement a cure: being *proactive* automatically slows down time and puts it back in our control.

TWO TYPES OF MOMENTUM: PROACTIVE AND REACTIVE

As a coach, I spend a lot of time watching how salespeople work, observing their sales momentum. I've found that no matter what their sales environment or structure, there are only two types of momentum: proactive and reactive. And the amount of time you spend in one mode rather than the other has a lot to do with your sales success.

Some startling statistics indicate that the average salesperson actually sells for only ninety minutes per day—per very *long* day— because they spend the majority of their time on highly *reactive* tasks:

non-revenue-generating activities. A 2008 study by the Yankee Group found that salespeople spend only 26 percent of their average day selling. So it should come as no surprise that, in my training, we spend a lot of time discussing the difference between proactive tasks and reactive tasks.

The difference is easy to remember:

> ➤ Presales activities are *proactive.* When you are working on these tasks, you are in control of your time and you are working toward generating revenue.
> ➤ Postsales activities are *reactive.* When you are working on these tasks, someone else is controlling your time and your works does not correlate with sales.

For example, if you're configuring a system presales before a customer is ready to buy, this is proactive. But if you're doing it after the purchase, just to be helpful because the customer knows you, then you're wasting your valuable time.

Are You Reactive or Proactive?

The first step toward taking control of your time is to figure out how you are working right now and how your environment impacts you. Face it, we live and work in a reactive world. You may think your time is spent proactively, when in fact you are using up your precious day with non-revenue-generating activities. See how many of the following activities sound familiar.

Proactive activities include:

> ➤ Cold-calling new prospects
> ➤ Making introductions
> ➤ Following up on quotes
> ➤ Navigating to get key decision makers
> ➤ Building organizational charts

Reactive activities include:

> Answering e-mails
> Troubleshooting issues or problems
> Researching questions
> Cleaning out your inbox
> Building a new spreadsheet
> Talking with a field partner
> Entering notes into your database

Ten Ways to Be Proactive Right Now

Once you understand how to effectively differentiate between proactive and reactive tasks, it gets easier to make the switch. Here are some ideas for quick fixes:

1. Use your commuting and travel time efficiently. Read, make notes, prioritize activities, or plan your day.

2. Learn to qualify your prospects. Don't waste time pursuing bad leads.

3. Update your contact management program and keep it current. When you maintain updated records, you can easily assess information and integrate it into your call.

4. Ask for the first appointment of the day. It's the one most likely to start on time.

5. Rearrange your workspace using the "near-far" rule: Keep things you use frequently at arm's length, and place the things you don't use as often out of the way.

6. Don't waste time on unproductive chit-chat.

7. When you have a quick question or a short answer, call during lunch and leave it on voice mail. Be specific, so your prospect can respond with a complete, detailed answer.

8. Group your calls. Place a flurry of calls in the morning, and then block out time to do the work created by the calls, such as sending e-mail and getting answers. Repeat this step in the afternoon.

9. Set non-negotiable power calling hours and be proactive during peak calling times.

10. Associate with time-conscious, organized, and motivated sales-people. The feeling is contagious. They will spur you on to make the most out of your time.

REGAIN YOUR MOMENTUM

When we watch a great sales presentation or listen to an exceptional web demo, we measure its true success by the planning and preparation that takes place *before* the event and the follow-up that happens *after* the pitch. That's what momentum is: what happens before and after. Approaching time management with purpose and intention strengthens your momentum. The best way to start is by paying attention and focusing with your eyes wide open. This crisp awareness regulates your momentum.

Recapture Prioritization: Learn to Say "No"

In my training, I always ask people if they can think of someone who is really good at saying "no." Most people do.

When I ask what qualities make these people so good at saying "no," the most common response is that these individuals know how to prioritize and reprioritize to reject taking on others' responsibilities. They may give me an example of a top-performing manager who says "no" to new reports, new meetings, new training, and new programs. Many people get nervous when we have this discussion, because their perception of saying "no" is seen as refusing to do their job or rejecting a request. They feel uncomfortable because they already have such little control of their time that they can't imagine saying "no" to their manager, their field partner, or their peers.

In my experience, people who have a hard time saying "no" also have unrealistic estimates of the time it takes to carry out a task. They don't want to offend others, they want to belong, and they want to be in demand. They thus get caught up in the assumptions they believe others have of them.

If this sounds familiar, take heart. Saying "no" doesn't mean you should refuse a task; it means you just need to be selective. Setting expectations, learning how to prioritize, and negotiating are all part of saying "no." Not all tasks need to be done, and not all tasks need to be handled immediately. Learn how to say "no" to a less important task that takes away from your sales momentum. Learn how to say "no" to a task you're told must be handled immediately and reprioritize that task for a later time in the day.

Learn to apply the following actions to requests for time you don't really have to spare:

> *Control interruptions.* This is especially important during your power calling hours. Don't take unscheduled meetings, let voice mail get your calls, and save socializing for later.

> *Say no to the request, not to the person.* Suggest an alternative, such as, "I can't do X right now, but I can do Y this afternoon." Avoid using negative words like "impossible," "incapable," "mistaken," "overloaded," or "ridiculous." And thank the person for thinking of you!

> *Remember your priorities.* The best reason for saying "no" is interference with your own priorities. Keep these priorities foremost in your mind, and articulate them to others. Refuse to spread yourself too thin, especially when your capabilities are in demand!

> *Delegate more effectively.* Define the task clearly, define accountability, communicate clearly, give feedback, don't get in the way, and reward effort and results.

> *Ask questions.* Without saying "yes" or "no," ask more qualification questions to help you better understand the request and to set expectations. Remember not to dwell on your needs or wants.

Adopting new efficient time management habits is not as easy as it seems, especially when you are in reactive mode and can barely hold your head above water. Good time management habits take time to implement—and that's exactly what the problem is about, loss of time. In my many years of training inside sales team members, I have found that when they just try one new idea it makes a big difference in their ability to control their time and, ultimately, their commissions.

Recapture Planning

The secret to properly managing your time lies in the choices you make. When you're in frantic mode, as Susan was at the beginning of this chapter—it's a great big clue that you haven't stepped back to look at where all your time is going, or to plan how to use your time proactively. When you work according to a thoughtfully determined plan, however, you can relax in the knowledge that you are exactly where you need to be and doing what you need to be doing. When you take the time to plan and set goals, it allows you time to actualize your vision, understand what may hold you back, and determine how to get there.

When a salesperson is assigned a territory, it only makes sense that they take the time to really understand that universe. But when territories are reassigned each quarter, customers change, products change, and markets change, so it's no wonder that territory planning may not be a priority. Yet the simple exercise of mapping out goals and account strategies, and highlighting a target list of top twenty-five accounts, helps the salesperson focus. And that pays off. Remember not to get so attached to your plan. Flexibility is key for an inside salesperson. Being rigid with your plan will only cause you to be more frustrated, angry, and resentful. An *adjustable* plan, in contrast, will help you be steady in a wobbly situation.

Let's start with the two biggest planning categories: territory planning and activity planning. One is strategic (territory) and one is more tactical (activity) planning.

Strategic Territory Planning. The more you know about your geographical region, the more you can penetrate it strategically and proactively. A Territory Plan ensures you are on the same page with your managers and field partners and establishes a "we are in this together" attitude. Many successful inside sales team members design a quarterly Territory Plan, which they revisit, refine, and refresh on a regular basis. This helps managers and sales team members synchronize their efforts. This Territory Plan becomes the roadmap for your sales goals. It includes some of the following:

> *Sales revenue goals*: YTD, annual, quarterly, monthly, daily
> *Top twenty-five target account list*: top strategic accounts you have identified as target accounts you would like to penetrate
> *Account base ranking*: organization and review of your current account base to determine how each customer or prospect ranks
  • High maintenance/low profit
  • High maintenance/high profit
  • Low maintenance/low profit
  • Low maintenance/high profit
> *Territory summary and overview*: what is happening in your region
> *Trends and early adopters*: what target customer is quick to adopt your solution
> *Competitive profile and market share*: what the competitive landscape looks like
> *General SWOT analysis*: analysis of your strengths, weaknesses opportunities, and threats, and where you might be blindsided

Tactical Activity Planning. You know the drill when you start out in inside sales: you're given a quota, told to make twenty-five to seventy-five outbound calls per day, set appointments, hand over leads, or close opportunities. You can accomplish these tasks successfully if you take the time to design an Activity Plan.

The most successful salespeople put a value on their time. They know they must hit a certain number of sales activities to measure their day's worth and they understand what it takes to reach it. Remember, sales is still a numbers game. Your Activity Plan will help you determine the daily, weekly, and monthly requirements you need to reach your goals.

Here are some questions to think about as you put your Activity Plan together:

> ➤ How long is your sales cycle?
> ➤ What is your conversion rate from a lead to an oppor demo to a presentation? From a presentation to a quote? From a quote to a closed opportunity?
> ➤ How many outbound calls will you make per day? The connection rate is roughly 8 percent, so if you make fifty-five outbound calls per day, chances are that you will connect with only four or five prospects. And when you do connect, how qualified will they be?
> ➤ How many presentations or demos do you have to make per week?

Your Activity Plan might look something like this:

> ➤ Thirty-five outbound calls per day
> ➤ Five high-level, meaningful conversations per day
> ➤ Fifteen new e-mail introductions per day
> ➤ Five demo/web presentations per week
> ➤ Five new partner calls per week
> ➤ Three conference calls per week
> ➤ Three new quotes/proposals per week

Recapture Phone Control: Set Non-Negotiable Power Calling Hours

You may find yourself beginning each day with the best intentions for making new calls. But after checking e-mail, responding to messages, and attending a team meeting, the day has flown by. What went wrong? Inside sales requires courage, energy, focus, organization, and strategy. This means preparing mentally, emotionally, and physically, and setting *non-negotiable calling time.* Dedicating time to create new opportunities is critical. You must learn to set this time and stick to it.

Everyone has "power calling" hours, during which they feel the most comfortable making new calls. If you want to create new opportunities, increase your lead flow and revenue numbers, and grow your pipeline, setting non-negotiable time each day—preferably during your personal power calling hours—is your answer. Here's how it works:

> Determine the time when you have the most energy to make outbound calls. This can be early in the morning for some or early in the afternoon for others.

> Block out two hours for power calling. Any less, and you'll never get to it; any more, it becomes overwhelming.

> "Non-negotiable" means exactly that: you have to do it. You can't delay it for a meeting, a coworker's birthday party, or a coffee break. You must be proactive during this time, and it's non-negotiable to be reactive.

> Be prepared—mentally, emotionally, and physically—to pound the phone for a few hours.

> Prepare your tools, job aids, voice mail scripts, e-mail templates, and CRM (Customer Relationship Management) tool.

> Tell everyone about it. Hang up signs that read "9:00–11:00 a.m. is my power calling time" or "7:00–9:00 a.m. is my $$$ time" or "6:30–8:30 a.m. are my golden hours." You will get more respect and support from those around you who might otherwise be tempted to interrupt.

> Stick to these hours at least three times per week for one month. You'll see results.

Recapture E-Mail Control: Build an E-Mail Template Library

If you are spending more than six minutes crafting a single e-mail, you are probably not working efficiently. Why reinvent the wheel every time you send a correspondence? Design a library of strong e-mail templates you can use again and again. Chapter 2 will provide you with twenty suggested e-mail templates you can access throughout your sales cycle.

Recapture Messaging Control: Determine a Call Objective and Gain Commitment

Wait! Before you make that call, ask yourself: What is your call objective (what would you like to have happen as a result of making your call)?

Call Objectives. When call-connect rates are dropping, it's important to get the most out of each call by engaging in meaningful conversations. Focusing mentally *before* you make the call is a good start, and the best way to do it is to have a clear call objective. If you have a weak call objective, you will waste time and fail to get much accomplished. Taking the time to determine a clear and strong call objective before making a call is actually a time saver in the long run. It not only earns you time and purpose but helps you mentally decide how much time you really deserve to have.

Take a look at the weak and strong call objectives below, and make sure you know the difference!

Weak call objectives:
- ➤ I'm going to ask for their address so I can send them literature.
- ➤ I'm going to call to introduce myself to the territory.
- ➤ I'm going to check if he received the quote I sent.
- ➤ I'm going to ask to stay on their radar.
- ➤ I'm going to just touch base as a courtesy.

Strong call objectives:
- ➤ I'm going to close this quote.
- ➤ I'm going to learn more about the political hierarchy within the organization.
- ➤ I'm going to call to determine the virtual team I can assemble for this potential opportunity.
- ➤ I'm going to get a definite commitment on the paperwork.
- ➤ I'm going to up-sell the opportunity and create a compelling event.
- ➤ I'm going to identify the decision process, timeframe, requirements, and budget, and then ask for the business.
- ➤ I'm going to ask how the paperwork is coming along.

Wait Before Hanging Up. I'm convinced that most salespeople are working way too hard. They spend too much time focused on their agenda and on what they will do to move the sale forward. One way to reduce your load is to gain a commitment before you hang up from each call. Today, everyone seems to respond best when they are being held accountable for something. If you gain commitment before hanging up, this sets you up for future calls. When you set a clear call objective, gain momentum to move the call along. This will help earn time in the next calls.

Too often salespeople end calls with a weak but comfortable close, such as:

"I'll write up . . ."

"I'll send you . . ."

"I'll call you . . ."

They are often uncomfortable closing more definitively, so they end calls without having the next step in place.

Before ending every call, make sure you articulate the next steps. This should include an action step *you* will take and an action step *they* will take. Here are two examples:

1. *When the prospect wants you to call them back in two weeks*: "Sure, Bob, I'll call you back in two weeks. In the meantime, could you invite a few people from your team to be on that call?"

2. *When the prospect wants you to send them information before scheduling an appointment*: "Sure, Bob, I'm happy to send you information. What specifically would you like me to send you? And once I send it, can you prepare some questions we can discuss for our next call?"

Recapture Tool Control

It's time to add one of the most important activities to your calendar: learning tools. If you want to become more marketable as an inside salesperson, you need to take time to master your tools. Stop complaining about the tools you don't have, and start efficiently utilizing the ones you *do* have. Remember: they justify your sales existence, because when you leave, you are only as good as the sales you closed and the tools you utilized.

A 2007 survey conducted by CSO Insights on Improving Inside Sales Effectiveness Using Technology found a correlation between quota attainment and the use of more online tools. More tools incorporated into the sales cycle help to increase the effectiveness and efficiency of inside sales reps.

Be proactive—learn how to incorporate tools throughout the entire sales process. Prioritize, and invest most of your time on your CRM tool—which, in most cases, will probably be Salesforce.com—and your e-mail tool, which will probably be Outlook. Get better and better with these tools and break bad habits. Don't reinvent the wheel by designing complicated spreadsheets; work with what you have. Use them for contacts, calendaring, forecasting, proposals, and quotes.

Your company's website, blog, or intranet is also your main tool— that is, your online identity. Learn how to leverage it into your sales process, whether you are sending a white paper, inviting someone to a webinar, talking about the latest press release, or reading the latest case study by a platinum customer. You are the voice of that website to your customers.

Recapture Pipeline Control

Building a healthy pipeline is not a once-a-month activity. It should happen throughout the month, the quarter, the year. The best time to build a pipeline is when you are selling and closing business because your confidence, adrenaline, and messaging are up.

Recapture Lead Qualification Control: Moving It Through the Sales Funnel Faster

Building a healthy pipeline means adding qualified leads to the sales funnel. Establishing a strong qualification criterion is the first step. (We'll take a closer look at this in Chapter 3.)

Most salespeople are sluggish with their leads because they have not built a strong qualification map to help them quickly decide what to keep and what to toss. Instead, they waste time believing assumptions and listening with "happy ears" to something that isn't. We will discuss this more in future chapters.

TELEPHONE TECHNIQUES FOR MANAGING TIME

Time management isn't only about managing tasks. It also involves your vocal tone, pace, questioning, listening, closing, and prospecting behavior. Why? Because when you use effective phone techniques, you earn more time on the phone and reduce the span of the sales cycle.

The following is a list of dos and don'ts that will help you increase efficiency and reduce the sales cycle.

1. *Use an authoritative tone that demands attention.* A weak or questioning voice tone doesn't command attention or engage the listener.
   Don't: "Do you have time to talk? Do you mind if I ask you a few questions?"
   Do: "The timing is right for us to talk today."

2. *Speak at a quick pace to create urgency.* It's true—people from different parts of the country speak at varying speeds. You should certainly adjust for this—but remember that the quicker the pace, the faster you will get things done!
   Don't: "Hi, I'm, umm, wondering if you might have time to spend, um, with me on the phone now?"
   Do: "Glad I caught you today."

3. *Speak succinctly and check for understanding.* The key here is to ask trial closing questions rather than assuming that you're being understood. If you express yourself clearly and succinctly, you'll improve your chances of being understood and taken seriously.
   Don't: "I want to make sure I explain the new features with this 7.5 upgrade."
   Do: "How are you currently evaluating this solution?"

4. *Ask strong qualifying questions before presenting a solution. Set expectations.* Don't launch into your sales pitch before uncovering and aligning with the need.
   Don't: "I understand you are working on a CRM initiative that will impact your SFA goals, and that's how our Unified Communications will enhance your LCS and IM direction."
   Do: "What's your familiarity with our suite of products?"

5. *Ask for less time.* The days of asking for sixty-minute meetings are gone. Ask for less time and earn more.

Don't: "Can we meet next week for one hour to discuss your needs and learn about your environment?"

Do: "How's fifteen minutes on your calendar next week?"

6. *Demonstrate strong listening through information integration.* When you carry information to the table, you have a better chance of leaving with more than you brought. Meeting prospects halfway makes business faster and easier.

Don't: "I'm calling because you asked me to check back in two months."

Do: "Last time we spoke, you mentioned that you'd be looking into implementing this solution. I sent you a few white papers and would like to discuss any questions you have."

7. *Explain your solution succinctly.* When you are tasked with selling too many solutions, you risk overwhelming and confusing the prospect with too much information.

Don't: "Our LoadRunner includes game-changing technology that reduces the script creation process down to a few simple mouse clicks. Web (Click and Script) for LoadRunner enables you to record scripts at a higher presentation layer. It automatically captures the most valuable scripting information to create succinct, intuitive, and self-explanatory scripts, reducing scripting time and maintenance by an average of 80 percent."

Do: "What is your familiarity with game-changing technology?"

8. *Call high and speak with decision makers who have both influence and authority.* Too many salespeople waste time with people who usually say "no" or don't have the power to say "yes." Contacting the decision makers dramatically shortens the sales cycle.

Don't: "Did you get to meet with your boss last week to discuss the quote?"

Do: "Hi Bob, I appreciate your time on this call. I've been working closely with Jim and have a deep understanding of your current challenges in deploying new technology. We've designed an extensive solution to meet your short- and long-term needs. Did Jim present and review our quote with you last week?"

9. *Set action steps and gain commitment before hanging up.* It's important to use every call to set up the next call. That makes the difference between the twelve-month call cycle and the three-month cycle.

Don't: "When can I call you back?"

Do: "I'll send you a trial evaluation and call you after fourteen days, when it expires. At that time, we can discuss any new questions that came up. How does the morning of January 18 look for you?"

10. *Say "no" or push back on consultants, field partners, and internal customers who may take up too much of your time.* Learn to be self-disciplined and avoid interruptions. If you don't, "time bombs" will hinder your sales efforts.

    Don't: "Sure, I'll bring you up to speed on the meeting you missed."

    Do: "I entered all the notes into Salesforce. Why don't you review them and call me back to discuss?"

─────────────── **Time Management Reality Check**───────────────

If you're still struggling with time management, at least one of these inside sales warrior stories may resonate with you. Read on for some coaching solutions.

Too-Technical Bob: Bob is excellent at establishing rapport and gains trust immediately on each call. But his style tends toward the technical, and he doesn't have a strong sense of urgency or focus. It's not unusual for Bob to hang up from a call with plenty of information—but little of it is useful in moving the sale along.

Reality Check: No matter how great Bob's initial rapport, if he gets too technical he may lose his listener or spend time talking with someone who doesn't have the power to buy. Bob needs to anchor himself with a checklist of qualified questions, and use them to maintain control and move the call along. He must also set a time limit for calls—whether it's four minutes or twelve minutes—and stick to it.

Overly Organized Sylvie: Sylvie is very analytical and detailed. She carefully researches each prospect before making a call. She's also very organized, and wants all the right scripts nearby before she starts dialing. Creative and ambitious, she takes time out to design a new forecasting spreadsheet, new competitive collateral, and new price comparisons for each prospect. Everyone is thrilled with Sylvie's contributions, but all of this prep keeps Sylvie off the phone.

Reality Check: Sylvie needs to understand that all this detail work is actually slowing her down. In fact, she may be using research as a tactic to avoid making calls. Although it may be hard for her to let go of some of that great information, once she is able to redirect her energies to making calls and generating opportunities, she will be more successful.

Sloppy John: John is what most people think of as a "typical" salesperson. He's very brave and likes to shoot from the hip. He's funny, social, motivated, and engages very well. But ask John for his forecast, and he's always late with his numbers. Ask him to build a territory analysis, and it's sloppy—and scary. Review the notes fields on his CRM tool, and there's no data. Basically, John doesn't leave any tracks.

Reality Check: Any sales organization would love John's energy, determination, and courage. But John is actually doing his company a disservice because he isn't building or managing an information trail—critical for inside sales. If you don't have an information base, you have to duplicate efforts to build one. Focus is key here. Until John takes a step back to plan a success formula and prioritize his strategy *before* engaging with prospects, he may be heading toward a spectacular flameout.

TIME MANAGEMENT STRATEGIES

Effective time management is critical to effective inside sales. It begins with a daily, weekly, and monthly plan and extends through the entire sales cycle, affecting not only how you spend your time, but how you pace your calls and whether you meet your numbers. The good news? Even a few changes in how you manage time can result in a big positive shift, and success will encourage you to make more changes. The more you practice these skills, the easier they get. Over time, you'll discover your rhythm, and you'll learn the tricks that work the best for you.

1. Remember: There is a direct correlation between time control and quota control. Learn to use time to your best advantage.

2. Sales 2.0 overload has created more frustrated inside salespeople who complain of less time control and that they are overwhelmed with data, demands, and deadlines.

3. Time paralysis settles in as interruptions and distractions take their toll. It can take many forms, including phone, e-mail, messaging, lead management, tools, prioritization, power, pipeline, and planning paralysis.

4. Freedom comes when we recapture our time by learning to better differentiate between the proactive and reactive—and learning how to say "no" to the reactive. The fun begins as we learn how to create strategic and tactical plans that help us prioritize our business.

5. Get a momentum boost by setting non-negotiable power calling times during the week. This is guaranteed to make you money and create new opportunities. Stronger phone and e-mail control will support your momentum and build good habits.

6. Be ambitious with your call objectives so you can accomplish more from each call, and remember to gain commitment before hanging up. *Take the time to hold your prospects accountable by agreeing on something you will be doing and something they will be doing before your next call.*

7. Your new mantra is "Learn my tools, learn my tools, learn my tools." Don't forget to pick a few and learn them well, instead of trying too many and being sloppy. Especially important: your CRM and Outlook tools.

8. Pick up momentum in building a healthy sales funnel. Build your pipeline each week during the month rather than waiting until the adrenaline kicks in—because I guarantee you will not make the best decisions on that kind of fuel.

9. Your voice gives clues to others on how you manage your time. Learn to speak succinctly at a strong pace that creates urgency and invites people to respond quickly.

10. Remember: If you fail to plan, you plan to fail. Recapture your time control through good planning.

CHAPTER 2

INTRODUCING
Selling in Sound Bites

In this business, by the time you realize you're in trouble,
it's too late to save yourself. Unless you're running
scared all the time, you're gone.

—Bill Gates

In this chapter, you'll get valuable insight into:

- ⊘ Why your prospects decide to opt out during your introductions
- ⊘ Whether voice mail and cold-calling are dead or alive
- ⊘ Learning informed prospecting habits by utilizing tools
- ⊘ The necessity for multiple touches in your prospecting efforts
- ⊘ E-mail subject lines—what works today

You'll learn tools and tactics to help you:

- ⊘ Understand how Sales 2.0 trends are impacting messaging etiquette
- ⊘ Combine e-mail and voice mail messaging for a dynamic one-two introduction
- ⊘ Discover the important components in e-mail messaging
- ⊘ Learn to stay ahead of trends in e-mail
- ⊘ Identify strong opening probes that initiate a call and invite the prospect to talk

"Hi, this is Erin Skinner at Technomatic. We're the global leaders in the integrated solutions management space and I left you a voice mail and sent you an e-mail last week that I would like to follow up on. I'd like to schedule a call with you to introduce you to our full range of products and tell you how we can save you time and money. Please call at your convenience. Thanks."

"Hello, is this Tom Smith? Do you have a minute? Are you the person who makes decisions on security initiatives? Is this a good time to talk? You sound busy. I'm calling to follow up on a white paper you recently downloaded."

"Hi Betsy, I've been trying to reach you but have been unsuccessful. Please let me know if you might be interested in meeting with my field partner who will be traveling to your area next week. I look forward to hearing from you."

"Hi Susan, this is Joanne again calling to invite you and your staff to our upcoming webinar. It will be a sixty-minute presentation by our executive team on the future of branded technology. Can we sign you up?"

"Jamie! This is John with ABC Technologies. You may not know me but . . ."

. . . .

Hello? Is anyone there? Is anyone listening? Has the quality of your introduction earned you enough time to make anyone care?

INTRODUCING IS YOUR MOMENT OF TRUTH

You average forty to fifty outbound calls and e-mails per day, hoping for a connect rate of just 6 to 8 percent. You've got four seconds to make a good impression with your e-mail. When you finally get a live contact, you have only seven to fifteen seconds to make an introduction. If your contact likes what he or she hears, you earn more time to make your pitch. If not, you get slammed into sales prison with no one to bail you out.

Traditionally, inside salespeople have owned the beginning of the sales cycle: they are the front line and provide the introduction. The introduction is the key moment of truth for every salesperson. Why? Because a prospect's gut response to you—good, bad, or indifferent—

can determine the entire course of the sale. This means the impression you make on the phone and online is crucial to your success. But in today's noisy marketplace, when cold-calling and voice mail messaging are regarded as spam, it's essential to know the tricks and techniques that help you stand out and earn time.

THE SALES 2.0 OPT-OUT CROWD:
SELLING IN A RISK-AVERSE MARKETPLACE

Welcome to selling to the opt-out crowd—the distracted, busy decision makers who are bombarded with messages coming from every direction and in more forms than ever before. They listen in sound bites, review your messages through two-inch PDA screens, and ask that you *not* leave them a voice mail message because it will quickly be deleted. Overloaded inboxes and voice mail spammers have created prospects that have lost tolerance with first-time introductions. They believe that voice mail and cold-calling are out, and they've convinced a lot of inside salespeople of the same thing. On top of that, today's increasingly uncertain economic climate has created risk-adverse buyers who are looking for reasons to opt out.

Today's shut-out factor has gotten so rigid that salespeople rarely hear a live human voice. A typical call to a company can sound something like this:

> Thanks for calling ABC Company. Please listen to our menu of options. If you know the name or extension of the person you are trying to reach, press 1. . . . ring. . . . ring . . . ring. . . . Please leave a message and someone will return your call.

Then you hit the "0" or "#" key to try to get a human on the phone, only to hear "the option you have selected is invalid, please select again."

All of this creates extreme pressure for an inside salesperson, whose key role is to stand out immediately by demonstrating value with their messaging. In this climate, making a new introductory phone call is not only frustrating, it can actually be painful! In fact, I am convinced that so many introductions are sloppy simply because salespeople are fearful about leaving them.

Cold-Calling: Dead or Alive?

Quite a few reps bail on prospecting and cold-calling—tasks that practically define an inside salesperson—for another reason altogether: a generational belief that it's a waste of time. Most inside salespeople today are young members of Generation Y, also called "Millennials," born after 1980. They are eighty million strong, spend an estimated $200 billion a year, and have been raised on Facebook. They're technically astute, have little patience for things they deem a waste of time, and put a high value on work that they feel has meaning. They grew up with Web 2.0, are very comfortable using instant messaging, texting, and e-mail, and believe in the value of maintaining relationships online. They've opted out of cold-calling and using the phone because they feel that "spamming" their prospects and continually getting shut out is both rude and a waste of time. They like speed and believe in faster response, which is why they also believe that voice mail is dead.

But cold-calling, despite what you may believe, is very much alive. It's the old approach that's dead.

Cold-Calling Works—If You Do It Right

Many books and articles have been written about the death of cold-calling. Yet a 2008 Email Marketing Benchmark Guide, by MarketingSherpa, found that 30 to 50 percent of buyers said that as a result of a "cold call" they took an action that benefited the caller (such as attending a webinar or adding the vendor to their consideration for a purchase).

When you're selling in a Sales 2.0 environment, it's important to analyze how your customer wants to receive your message and determine the best way to send it. As Brian Carroll, author of *Lead Generation for the Complex Sale*, writes in his B2B Lead Generation blog, "Time and time again it is proven that customers want the salespeople they deal with to understand their business, their needs, and the pressures under which they operate. These people are called trusted advisors." When top decision makers who manage large budgets were asked what they considered to be strong sales introductions, they knew exactly what they did and did not want to hear on both voice mail and e-mail. Here are some examples of what they said:

> "Someone who has done their homework and knows about my company."
> "When a salesperson sounds professional, succinct, confident, and provides value with their message, I will listen to it."
> "I delete so many messages a day and the only thing that stands out for me is a strong, short personalized message that gets to the point."
> "I don't want to receive a prospecting call on my cell phone; that is an instant turn-off."

The bar for salespeople has been raised. Ignorant cold-calling—dialing executives without getting background on them, their company, or their challenges—is dead. But informed prospecting—where salespeople use Sales 2.0 tools like Hoover's, Jigsaw, Google, Facebook, and LinkedIn to make well-prepared and highly targeted calls—is alive and kicking.

A 2008 study conducted by Jigsaw, a provider of business information and data services, confirms this. In a survey of over seven thousand business professionals, it was found that their use of research tools helped drive 10 to 50 percent increases in productivity. The Sales 2.0 environment gives us a lot of great tools to use to research companies, and to incorporate interest and information into our introductions. Sales 2.0 tools approach messaging from both a sales and marketing perspective. That means sales reps must abandon old cold-calling tactics and integrate a solid marketing system into their overall strategy. Tracking your outbound messages through e-mail marketing tools will give you insight as to who is opening your messages and what they are doing with them.

New tools have also opened up possibilities and created new expectations for response time. Once a phone call was quicker than a letter, and face-to-face was quicker than a phone call. Now e-mail is quicker than face-to-face, and texting is the fastest way to get a response. In the next few years, mobile messaging will gain in importance and will become more incorporated into the sales process, because it contains some of the essential components of marketing and sales, such as speed, word choice, and short messages. Today, three billion people own cell phones, and more than one trillion text messages are sent every year. Texting has become an international phenomenon and will soon gain greater acceptance on a business level.

There's No Excuse for Not Doing Your Homework

It's rare today for a prospect to ask, "Where did you get my name or number?" because so much information is made public. With all the search tools you can call on, prospects expect your introduction to be personal and informed—not generic.

You can become an online sleuth and, *before* you make an introductory call to a target company, make sure you've done your homework. Start by searching through your Salesforce.com sales automation tool to see what previous history is available or if anyone from the target company has attended a webinar. Then search through the company's website to see what new product releases have been announced, or if any new partnerships or acquisitions are in the works. You can also read the CEO's blog, if one is available, to get a more personalized perspective. Next, you may want to dig through precall research tools such as Google, Hoover's, or Jigsaw to find more names within the target company and start figuring out who may be involved in the decision-making process there (we'll talk about this at length in Chapter 3, "Navigating"). Don't forget to include some social networking tools in your search such as LinkedIn, Facebook, YouTube, and Twitter as they provide real-time insights on your prospects.

You can customize an electronic business card with a few slides and combine that with audio recording attached to your email and send a two-minute introductory recording that may sound like this:

> Hi, Phil. This is Jessica with ABC Company and I'm eager to speak with you. I understand you recently announced a partnership with

Dava Corp—one of our preferred partners. In reading your CEO's blog, I noticed his priority this year is expanding your reach into new global markets. We are the premier solutions provider for access management, which is a good fit with the size and scope of your company. I'd like to request a few minutes of your time and invite some of your team members, such as Jack Cox, Brian Haffer, and Lisa Bentley, to join in. I'm happy to share the latest trends and research to prove our viability in the global marketplace. It would also be great to share stories about our glory years—I'm also a UC Berkeley alumnus. My contact information is attached in the e-mail I'm sending to back up this call. I look forward to speaking with you.

Reevaluating Introductions for Sales 2.0

The Sales 2.0 landscape has shaken sales to its roots, and has forced us to reevaluate our message strategies, tools, and responses. Inside salespeople are working with limited resources. No one really cares how great you look if they can't see you over the phone or in your messaging. In both e-mail and phone calls, it's your tone, pace, word choice, and organization that will get your foot in the door, earning you a call back or encouraging a prospect to open your e-mail.

This brings us back to the subject of this chapter: introducing yourself and your solution. Whether you've got a live person on the phone, you're leaving a voice mail, or you're sending a message, the importance of what you say and how you say it can never be underestimated or left to chance.

MAKING A LIVE PHONE CALL

I'm a very impatient salesperson—I believe getting live voices on the phone is always the best way to go. When you run up against a phone menu system designed to keep you out, pressing the "0" or "#" key will almost always redirect you out to a live contact.

Once you get an actual human being on the phone, don't be caught with nothing to say. Prepare a strong opening statement and keep it on hand. When you finally connect with a live voice, you'll be glad you did.

Opening statements can create objections very early on in the call. Prospects will say they have no time, must run to a meeting, or give the excuse that someone has just stepped into their office. Learn from adversity—paying attention to what gets you shut out early will give you a good indicator of what you need to improve on.

The one question salespeople always ask me about opening statements is this: "Should I ask them if they have a minute?" My answer is that your voice tone is key. If you have a strong tone, you can get away with asking if they have a few minutes to talk because they will be compelled to listen. A weak tone will automatically cause them to shut you out.

You don't have to listen to a recording to know which of the openings below will get the person to talk to you. Review the following strong and weak openings to understand the differences:

Weak:
- ➤ "I know I caught you at a bad time but I was thinking you might be interested in our . . ."
- ➤ "You sound pretty busy, so I can call you back."

Strong:
- ➤ "I'll be brief."
- ➤ "I'm glad to catch you . . ."

Weak:
- ➤ "This is a courtesy call, do you have a minute to talk or is this not a good time?"

Strong:
- ➤ "Glad I caught you today! I want to introduce myself—I'm part of the integrated sales team."

Weak:
- ➤ "I was calling to check if you had any projects or initiatives you were currently working on."

Strong:

> ➤ "I would like to introduce myself, check your familiarity with our company, and learn more about your department to see if there may be a match for our solution."

Weak:

> ➤ "Today we are calling on all of our wireless customers and your name came up on my database. Are you familiar with our suite of products?"

Strong:

> ➤ "I learned you are moving into a virtual sales organization and wanted to check your knowledge on our wireless solutions."

Voice Mail: Dead or Alive?

In 2008, Michael Arrington, founder of TechCrunch, a weblog dedicated to profiling and reviewing new Internet products and companies, surveyed his readers, asking if anyone was still using voice mail and if it was a necessary evil. After receiving an overwhelming anti-voice-mail response from his tech-centric audience, he wrote an article titled "Think Before You Leave Voicemail" and pleaded, "Voicemail is dead. Please tell everyone so they'll stop using it."

I agree that voice mail is considered a rude interruption, a stalking mechanism, a waste of time, and a tool that blocks you from getting in. Long voice mails are immediately deleted, confusing voice mails are considered spam, and automated voice mails are considered rude.

So: Is voice mail dead or alive?

Yes and no. I believe voice mail can no longer stand alone. And as much as your prospects hate receiving them, salespeople hate leaving them. When I hear inside salespeople say, "I don't leave voice mail messages anymore," I want to agree. But I can't. Why? Because I still believe people are in their offices when your call comes through. And because while there is no room for generic-sounding techno-blabbing or acronym-loaded voice mail messages, carefully crafted thirty-second voice mails that include a "what's in it for me" hook are not immediately deleted. In fact, I recently landed one of my biggest clients by leaving one simple voice mail message—followed by an e-mail.

THE MULTIPLE-TOUCH RULE

Research indicates that most salespeople give up trying to reach a prospect after four calls. Too bad, because research also indicates that an executive will only be receptive to talking with you after seeing your message *at least nine times*. In the real world, with low connect rates, it can take an average of *twenty-seven attempts* to gain a qualified appointment with a prospect. Hence, the "multiple-touch" rule.

In larger, complex sales, the number of times you must "touch" a prospect averages eight to twelve. To avoid overkill, each touch must be unique—you can't send the same message in the same way over and over. As John Jantsch, author of the Duct Tape Marketing Blog, explains, "Buyers like to receive information in many different ways. Some listen, some watch, some interact, some read, some lurk, and some react for no apparent reason at all." He continues to recommend that reps "develop a core marketing message and then deliver it in as many forms, mediums, and channels as possible. Your marketing and lead generation should be developed in ways that allow you to be seen on the Internet, in print, in video, in audio." He concludes, "When you develop this type of multi-foundational approach to your marketing you will find that your leads come to you more qualified and from many different places."

The multiple-touch rule reinforces the multi-foundational approach, which encourages you to utilize several introductory vehicles—phone, e-mail, and so on. Each contact not only has a unique value proposition, but also has a unique message. Be sure this message includes answers to the five W's (who, what, when, where, why) and the H (how):

Whom are you calling or writing to?

What is your purpose?

When are you sending the message?

Where do you expect them to receive the message?

Why are you sending the e-mail?

How do you want your prospect to respond?

Always remember everyone's favorite radio station, *WIIFM*, which stands for "What's in it for me?" Make sure to include a benefit.

Here's an example of a multi-foundational approach that uses various media forms to create an introduction:

> - Introductory voice mail (phone)
> - Introductory e-mail (e-mail)
> - Electronic business card e-mail (e-mail and audio)
> - Video introduction e-mail (visual, audio, e-mail)
> - Webinar invitation from marketing (e-mail)
> - Webinar voice and e-mail follow-up (e-mail and voice mail)
> - New product release from marketing (e-mail)
> - New case study with video link to customer demo (e-mail)
> - Competitive benchmark with a free trial evaluation (e-mail)
> - Proposal request with new pricing and incentives (e-mail)

Voice mail? Yes, that's the first bullet on the list. If you thought voice mail was in the same outbox as cold-calling, think again.

THE DYNAMIC DUO: VOICE MAIL + E-MAIL

Meet the new power couple. No, it's not Angelina Jolie and Brad Pitt or David and Victoria Beckham. It's the marriage of the Dynamic Duo: e-mail and voice mail. Even if voice mail is slowly dying, that doesn't mean it's time to stop leaving messages. It means your voice mail can't stand on its own. It needs a cohort—e-mail. These two are inseparable. They have so much in common, it's no wonder they make such a perfect match.

Here's an example of the Dynamic Duo at work:

Voice mail:

> Hi [First Name].
>
> This is {Your name and Company}. We are the leaders in {your solution} with over {xyz companies who rely on your solution}.
>
> The reason for my call is to schedule a brief meeting with you to learn more about your {customize} growing needs.
>
> Thanks. I look forward to speaking with you and can be reached at {your number}.

E-mail follow-up:

> Hi/Hello [First Name].
>
> I'm following up from my voice mail as I'm eager to speak with you in reference to {customize your solution}. I understand you are currently utilizing {include something you know about their organization} and I'd like to schedule a six-minute phone conversation within the next week to learn more about your needs and share the success of our application.
>
> {Name of your company} is the leader in {customize this}. More than 10,000 businesses in some of the fastest-growing Fortune 500 companies rely on our {your product or services} for their {customize their needs}. They have found we provide unparalleled results in the following areas:
>
> > Increase in {customize}
> >
> > Stronger in {customize}
> >
> > Reduction in {customize}
>
> I will follow up in a couple of days to confirm a time to discuss your {customize} needs.
>
> Thank you. I look forward to speaking with you!
>
> Your name
> Your company
> Office, cell, fax
> Web address
> Tagline

Once you've left these messages, remember to:

> *Follow up within minutes.* E-mail and voice mail must be submitted within minutes or even seconds of each other. That means you can't leave a voice mail and follow up that afternoon with an e-mail. Response drops when the two are not combined and synchronized.

> *Keep track of outbound e-mails.* When you are making new introductions, don't just count on your phone and voice mail efforts. If you are keeping track of outbound call metrics, you must also keep an eye on outbound e-mails.

TAKE E-MAIL CONTROL

There was a time when we relied on the marketing department to manage our e-mail requirements. They carefully crafted e-mails with tons of fluffy marketing words, created auto responders for incoming leads and web visits, and blasted our customer base on a regular basis. So where did that leave you? With tons of dirty data that needed scrubbing and lots of upset prospects!

Today, everyone is sending e-mail—not just marketing. According to the Carlson Marketing Group, 2.4 trillion e-mail messages are being sent annually in the United States. In a few years, e-mail penetration will reach 61 percent of all Americans. But something else has changed: *you* have control of the e-mail that goes to prospects.

⊘ According to one estimate, the WWW will produce 27 billion gigabytes of emails by 2010 and about 26.5 billion gigabytes of that e-mail will be poorly written! Since e-mail is to be the most cost-effective marketing and sales solution, taking control of it is key. Taking control of your e-mail means understanding it inside and out. I like to break e-mail into two broad categories: (1) the all-important subject line that hooks their attention, and (2) the e-mail content that pulls them in.

Good Subject Lines Generate Response

Today, the most important part of an e-mail is the subject line: the prospect doesn't have to read any further than that in order to know whether it's correspondence they will want to read or send straight to the trash. According to a 2007 study conducted by Juniper Research, 35 percent of e-mail users open messages because of what is contained in the subject line. The lesson? Make sure your subject lines work!

What's the Platform? It's important to understand how your e-mails are being received and reviewed. What browser? What smartphone? HTML or plain text? There are 2.5 million Blackberry users in the United States, and even more devices and platforms such as iPhone, Palm Treo, Microsoft® Outlook®, Gmail, Yahoo!, MSN, AOL, and Hotmail.

Subject Lines That Sell. A good subject line gets your e-mail opened and increases the chance of a response. According to the Marketing-Sherpa E-mail Marketing Benchmark 2008 Study, the top two challenges facing decision makers today are overstuffed mailboxes and the fact that spam has eroded trust. When inboxes are overloaded, it's more important than ever to craft good subject lines that get your e-mail read—not lines that land your e-mail in the spam filter.

Crafting good subject lines is an art. Orchestrating the right subject line that stands out, gets opened, and gets responded to is a skill. An excellent way to train your brain and your eye is to read newspaper headlines or online headlines at sites such as the Yahoo!, MSN, or AOL home pages. What do you see? You probably see a few key words, well placed. Just as these concise headlines get you to click and read the full article, using fewer (and the right!) words in subject lines leads to better open rates and ensures that prospects will read your message.

Keep your subject line short and to the point. This means no more than thirty-five characters, or no more than six words. Here are examples of both ineffective (overlong) and effective (concise) subject lines:

Weak: Latest White Paper on Distributed Computing Written by Jan Jacobs, Global Sales Operations
Strong: Global Trends on Distributed Computing

One secret to good subject lines is simply to combine your company name and your prospect's company name with a strong action verb. That way, when your prospect files your e-mail, they make a subconscious connection in partnering both companies. For instance:

Nimsoft beats McAfee's expectations

Lantec captures the HP Market

Gardner endorses Altiris in Magic Quadrant

E-Mail Templates and Recommended Subject Lines

Why reinvent the wheel every time you write an e-mail? Once you learn to create well-crafted e-mails that are relevant, timely, and personalized, you can easily repurpose them for new prospects simply by changing the details. The subject lines for your templates are templates too. Feel free to adapt the following to your own needs:

General Broad Product Suite Introduction
[YOUR COMPANY NAME] overview for [PROSPECT COMPANY NAME]

First Introduction and Contact Information
[YOUR COMPANY NAME] picks up speed with [PROSPECT COMPANY NAME]

Second Introduction
[YOUR COMPANY NAME] makes immediate impact with [PROSPECT COMPANY NAME]

Last Attempt/Tough to Reach/Before Your Close the Lead
It's not too Late for [PROSPECT COMPANY NAME] and [YOUR COMPANY NAME]

Request for appointment
Four minutes of your time?

Lead response; follow-up on webinar, white paper download
[YOUR COMPANY NAME] 06.12.08

Qualification
Are you ready for [YOUR COMPANY NAME]?

Competitive
Top three reasons why companies choose [YOUR COMPANY NAME] or four Big Reasons to an Alternative Solution to Security.

Invitation for Event or Demo
[YOUR COMPANY NAME]—*Bringing People, Processes, and Systems Together*
Register Today and Learn Five New Ways to Build Traffic

Pricing and services
[YOUR COMPANY NAME] Cost Estimates for [ABC Company]
[YOUR COMPANY NAME] Fee Structure for [ABC Company]
[YOUR COMPANY NAME] Brings Profitable Returns: 2008 Fee Structure for [ABC Company]

Proposal and Quote Delivery
Perfect Timing for [PROSPECT COMPANY NAME]

News and Announcement to Existing Customer Base
[YOUR COMPANY NAME] 2008 News and Alerts from [PROSPECT COMPANY NAME]

Title-specific
VP of Sales consistently endorses [YOUR COMPANY NAME]

Vertical-specific
[YOUR COMPANY NAME] paves the way in the financial sector with [PROSPECT COMPANY NAME]

Good E-Mail Messages Get to the Point and Deliver What the Prospect Needs

Once you've gotten a prospect's attention with the subject line, it's important to back it up with a great e-mail. That means not wasting their time making them figure out what you're trying to say and why they should care. Your opening sentence, your choice of words, a clear call to action all formatted for quick review invites response.

"Punch Out" Your Opening Sentence. I always tell my trainees to make sure they punch out the opening sentence of every e-mail. That means get to the point quickly and confidently about your e-mail's purpose:

> *Don't say:* I have been trying to call you to introduce myself over the phone but I have had no success, so I thought I would send you an e-mail. I was hoping to get on your calendar for a sixty-minute discovery call to discuss some information.

> *Do say:* As part of your dedicated Account Team, I would like to extend an invitation to review our Unified Communications vision and roadmap. With your current investment in Exchange, you already have one of the products in this mix.

Can you see the difference from the perspective of the prospect, who is wondering why should he or she engage with you? The first sample basically confirms you are not resourceful in making something happen, you lack confidence, and do not have anything specific other than taking up too much of their time. The second example identifies you, *and* says that you're part of their team and you have a solution just for them. Perfect!

Choose Strong Words. Your choice of words tells the listener volumes about your background, education level, age, and professionalism. In sales, short sentences and clear communication always win out over big words, long sentences, and complex ideas.

Think about the words you choose to use when you introduce yourself to a prospect:

> ➤ Are you so wordy that you confuse your listener?
> ➤ Are you hiding behind big, "impressive" words?

Let's look at two sample introductions that say the same thing. The only difference is in word choice: one uses more complicated language, the other is simple. Which one gets its point across better?

> *Complex language:* By providing the industry's only distributed transactional security infrastructure, our solution gives organiza-

tions the ability to create standard policies that can combine both static and dynamic rules, and change rules on the fly based on the needs of the business.

Simple language: Our company has grown steadily over the past ten years, attracting customers such as Disney, EDS, Ford, Apple, and others that rely on our enterprise solution. We provide our clients with striking results, including . . .

Which do you prefer? Most customers perceive the first introduction as deceptive. Rather than impressing the prospect, the use of multi-syllable words actually distances them, and leads them to believe you might be hiding something. The more straightforward introduction, on the other hand, is strongly worded and gets right to the point, leaving no doubt about who you are.

Make a Power Words Cheat Sheet

When you're trying to craft an opening statement or e-mail, it's very helpful to have a cheat sheet of active, clear words and phrases. Stay away from nonwords or weak words. Instead, include strong, results-oriented power words and phrases such as: *best-selling, successful, superior, improve, quality, ideal, accomplished, proven, results, performance, solution, special, unique, customized, powerful, more, stronger, growth, indispensable, expertise, niche, sophistication, specialize, new, latest, innovative, easy, effortless, simple, convenience, eliminate, less, fewer, speed, time-conscious, efficient, quickly, affordable, savings, accurate, precise, control, comprehensive, thorough, flexible, compatible, reliable, security, loyal, solid, support, satisfaction, replace.*

Also, keep in mind that some words have a life span and when they are overused, their true meaning becomes distorted. Let's look at an example from a high-tech company and the words they used for the past forty years in their marketing material:

> ➤ In the 1960s: hi-fi, transistor, Technicolor, space-age technology
> ➤ In the 1970s: quadraphonic, turbo-charged, supersonic, mainframe

> ➤ In the 1980s: microcomputer, telnet, surround sound, nerds, DOS
> ➤ In the 1990s: paradigm shift, information highway, e-commerce, Y2K
> ➤ In 2000: hit refresh, blogging, podcasting, next generation

Format. No matter how good your message is, if it's buried in a badly formatted paragraph, your prospect will never read it. You want to aim for something that is easy on the eyes and inviting.

Don't use:

- ➤ Long, blocky, wordy paragraphs. People with only seconds to give you don't want to spend them with their eyes crossed trying to figure out what you're saying.
- ➤ Brightly colored graphics. Pretty as you may think these are, they will only distract from your message.

Look at these two samples. Which one gets its point across?

> Our Enterprise Content management offering differs from the competition in three key ways. First, we have the only complete solution covering all key functionality areas: document management, content management, rich media management, site management, and content delivery. The competition only covers one or some combination of these areas and to a varying level of depth. A detailed analysis of our functionality vis-à-vis the competition will bear this out.

Or,

> **Enterprise Content Management key differentiators:**
>
> *Document Management* surpasses our competitors
> *Content Management continues to lead the way in scalability*
> *Rich Media Management* ties the entire package together

The second example is easier on the eyes. The bulleted list tells the prospect what's important, and invites the customer to read further.

No Long Attachments. Long attachments are a thing of the past for a very good reason: no one wants to open an attachment that comes in one unsolicited e-mail and end up with a malicious virus that crashes their system!

As an alternative, try embedding a few hyperlinks in your message. Inviting prospects to click on links is a quick and easy way to get them to go exactly where you want them to go—to learn more about your solution.

E-Mail Tone. Remember our discussion about voice tone when speaking on the telephone? Your e-mail tone is just as important. In e-mail, your tone is revealed in how you type your message and in the words you use.

A message written in ALL CAPS, or a message that uses **too much bold** is read as shouting—an immediate turnoff. Lots of exclamation marks!!! and emoticons ;-) can also annoy prospects, and are read as unprofessional.

Always remember to be professional in your tone. As we discussed earlier, this does not mean using big, impressive words, or using a lot of words. It does mean using language that is clear and respectful at all times.

Watch Out for Grammar and Typos. Being professional also means making sure you've checked your e-mail for poor grammar and typos or misspellings *before* you hit the Send key. A lack of awareness for these details will always trigger a negative impression about your intellect, professionalism, and attention to detail.

Think before pressing SEND:

> Thank you for your time of the the phone this morning. I have included general info on our compnay for your perusal. Please, contact me at 408-555-1212 if you hav any questions.

Do send this e-mail:

> Thank you for your time on the phone this morning. I have included general information on our company for your perusal. Please contact me at 408-555-1212 if you have any questions.

These two examples illustrate how a prospect can easily be put off with poor grammar and typos and will thus spend less time on the intent of the message.

Always End with an Action Step. If you want a response, always end your e-mail with an action step. This tells the prospect what they can do to learn more, and doesn't leave them wondering why you contacted them.

Weak:
> "Let me know if you have any questions, or if you would like a more in-depth discussion around these solutions, please don't hesitate to call."

Strong:
> "Please provide me with your availability in the next week for a brief meeting."
> "I look forward to speaking with you."

Keep Your Signature Line Short. Signature lines are getting colorful, busy, lengthy, and landing in spam filters. Many organizations' marketing departments require their employees to use their embedded logo in their signature lines along with a tagline and sometimes an upcoming event.

In addition to that, reps will add their name, title, region, addresses, mobile phone, office phone, Skype address, and fax. The result is that the signature line starts looking way too busy and bottom-heavy, and increases the chances of the e-mail landing in a spam filter because it is too media rich.

Before You Press "Send" Checklist

How many times have you hit the "Send" key without checking your e-mail and then regretted it the next second? Take a few minutes to review the following checklist before pressing Send the next time:

- ⊘ Will the subject heading get their attention?
- ⊘ Is the e-mail's tone inviting, interesting, trustworthy, and confident?
- ⊘ Is the e-mail's tone consistent with the tone of your voice mail message?
- ⊘ Does your thinking appear organized?
- ⊘ Is the e-mail too long?
- ⊘ Does the e-mail have unsolicited attachments?
- ⊘ Is the first sentence a "grabber"? Does the message arouse curiosity?
- ⊘ Does the message convey a purpose?
- ⊘ Do the words or phrases sound overused and contrived?
- ⊘ What's in it for them? What are the benefits?
- ⊘ Does the e-mail end with an action step for them to take?

Don't Get Sent to the Spam Filter! There is nothing more frustrating than taking the time to write a great e-mail, only to find it has landed in the spam filter because of your subject line. You can go a long way toward avoiding this fate by understanding what spam filters look for. Recently, an editor I know put the phrase "Writing Specialist" in her e-mail subject line and wondered why her e-mail was landing in everyone's spam filter. It turns out that when you look closely at the word "specialist," you see that it contains the word "CIALIS," which is a sex-enhancing drug spam filters automatically look for.

Becoming knowledgeable about spam filters is an ongoing task—rules change all the time as spam filters become more sophisticated. Some things, however, are Spam 101:

- ➤ No !@$#% SYMBOLS!
- ➤ No misspelled words or w0rd5 with numbers
- ➤ Words and terms to avoid:

Free, No Obligation, Offer, Limited Time, Deal, Sale, Pricing, Guarantee, Renewal, Just Released, Specials, Gift, Bargain, Marketing, Discount, Pleasure, Lowest Prices, Clearance, Final Day, Performance, Market, Bonus, Click, Advertising, Ads, Sell, Shopping, Package, Finance

Experiment with Send Times. When should you send your e-mails? Does it really matter?

Yes. According to MarketingSherpa's E-mail Marketing Benchmark 2008 Guide, people read e-mails at the same time they tend to be online. That's lunchtime. The majority of Internet users log on to do non-work-related activities during their lunch breaks from work.

Still, attempting to time your e-mails to match the natural usage patterns of Internet users can get confusing. Sending an e-mail on a Sunday doesn't mean that only 14 percent will read it; it just means that a lot more people will read it on Monday.

Experiment. Try different approaches, and make sure to measure the results. Test the subject line, the offer, the call to action, the day of the week, and the frequency. Remember to include an unsubscribe option; use your standard "opt-out" option, such as *"Reply to this message with Unsubscribe in the subject line if you no longer wish to receive e-mails from . . .".*

Writing E-Mails That Sell. *Before you begin* (state your objectives and know your audience).

1. *Punch out your opening sentence*: grab them in the first glance

2. *Choose strong words:* say what you mean

3. *Format and organize:* keep it clean—we'll dig into this in a bit

4. *Slow down on attachments:* unless they know they're coming

5. *Establish a tone:* this goes back to the beginning—know your audience and make sure they know you

6. *Watch for grammar and typos:* when all else fails, spell check

7. *End with an action step:* ensure a response

8. *Keep your signature line short:* six lines maximum

9. *Before you hit Send:* check your work against this list

10. *Understand what is tagged as spam or junk mail:* educate yourself and stay current on these always-changing rules

11. *Experiment with send times:* each day of the week makes a difference and remember that timing is everything

12. *Write killer subject headings:* these create interest and capture attention

──────────── **Have They Earned Time Reality Check**────────────

"All my prospects suck. They never call me back. They just give me some lame excuse. I'm really getting to hate this job!"

Some sales reps keep getting shut down. They just can't seem to get past their introductions, and they don't understand what they're doing wrong. It must be the client! But, of course, it's not. Here are some typical problems I see every day in my work with inside salespeople:

Exclusive E-Mails for Elaine: Elaine is convinced her customers see the phone as a big interruption, so her talk time is extremely low but her e-mails are high.

Reality Check: Elaine may feel more comfortable with e-mail, but she shouldn't give up on using the phone. No matter how much times have changed, the phone will always be inside sales' primary messaging medium—but it can no longer stand alone. It must work in concert with tools to support our phone efforts. Elaine must increase her phone activity to complement her e-mail efforts.

Growing-Stale Serena: Serena is so tired of leaving voice mail messages that her pitch sounds like a broken record. When she finally gets a live person on the phone, she comes across as robotic, frustrated, and very formal.

Reality Check: Prospects receive hundreds of calls from vendors. It's no wonder that they're sick of listening to generic, canned openings and voice mails. Serena needs to invest time in crafting unique introductions so she can stand out with her first impression. She must make it authentic, personalized, and unique.

Tricky Ted: Ted always gets call backs because he leaves very little information and asks to be called back immediately and believes that is why people call him back. His introduction may sound like this, "Hi, Bob, this is Ted and I need to speak with you in reference to a few things, please call me back."

Reality Check: Ted is starting off on the totally wrong foot. Tricking your prospects is a sure way to ruin any potential relationship you might have. Don't set unrealistic expectations with your prospects. Be professional and do not risk being tricky.

Timid Tracy: When Tracy worked as an executive assistant to a CEO, she screened a lot of calls from salespeople and has an inherent disrespect for cold-calling. Now that she's working in inside sales, she feels tentative about picking up the phone. She says she doesn't want to bother anyone—she feels like a telemarketer.

Reality Check: When we are prospecting business-to-business, we must remember it's the prospect's *job* to actually listen and review our solution. We are not calling them at home during dinner or on weekends after they've returned from their golf game, we are calling during appropriate business times.

INTRODUCING STRATEGIES

1. *Realize that first impressions are made within seconds.* Our telephone first impression is under fifteen seconds and our e-mail first impression is under three seconds. Make every second count.

2. *Personalize the message.* Pay attention to your prospects and put yourself in their shoes. They are becoming more intolerant of bland messaging but still interested in personalized and prepared messages.

3. *Do your homework.* Use all the great tools at your disposal to prepare more intelligent and informed introductions that will earn you more time.

4. *Stay on top of messaging trends.* Sales 2.0 has created a messaging evolution. Now we are expanding into new messaging options such as interactive business cards, video blogging, e-messaging, and digital voice mails.

5. *Acknowledge that voice mail is still alive.* Voice mail is still a significant messaging vehicle. Leave well-organized, short (thirty seconds or less) messages, and follow up right away with an e-mail.

6. *Go live.* Getting someone live on a call is still the best introduction. Having a strong opening statement ready to go can support that opportunity.

7. *Know that e-mail + voice mail = increased response.* This winning combination ensures a "double whammy" message that gets attention and increases your chance for response.

8. *Compile an e-mail template library.* This is the best investment of time you can make. Take time to design some solid e-mails you can repurpose and utilize throughout the sales cycle.

9. *Use subject lines that will get a response.* Be professional, creative, and succinct. Link your company name to theirs with an action verb that gets attention.

10. *Pay attention to changing e-mail rules.* Attachments are out, hyperlinks are in, and phrases such as "writing specialist" will land you in the spam filter. These are just a few e-mail rules you should know, and more rules are being added as you read this sentence! Keep current so your e-mail doesn't turn into junk mail.

CHAPTER 3

Navigating
Avoiding the No-Po's

We have been doing things that are contrary—the things people
tell us won't work from the beginning. In fact the only way to get
ahead is to find errors in conventional wisdom.

—Larry Ellison

In this chapter, you'll get valuable insight into:

- ⊘ Why you stay loyal to No-Po's who can't help you
- ⊘ Why it's in their best interest to keep you away from real power
- ⊘ Why software designed to help you find contacts in a company is often no help at all

You'll learn tools and tactics to help you:

- ⊘ Build an org chart that works
- ⊘ Understand the underlying political structures that influence the decision-making process in any organization
- ⊘ Discern whether particular gatekeepers can help or hurt the sales process
- ⊘ Determine who makes the buying decisions

I look at the sales rep's forecast, which hasn't moved for months, and ask the question: "Does your prospect really have the juice to buy?"

"Of course," Jeff replies. "Bob's a great guy. He's working hard for me on this."

"Then why do you think this deal has been stagnant for so long?"

Jeff doesn't miss a beat. Right away, he tells me that Bob's boss asked for more information, a big meeting had to be rescheduled, budget got reallocated at the last minute . . .

I interrupt the litany of excuses beyond his control. "How about if you call your prospect while I listen in?"

He agrees, and this is what I hear:

"Hi, Bob. It's Jeff—with Scroll Technologies"

"Oh, hey, Jeff. How are things going?"

"Great. I wanted to check—did you receive the competitive information I sent you yesterday?"

"Yeah, I haven't had a chance to look at it, but I appreciate you following up on it. Hey, I was just about to jump into a meeting when you called. How about if you call me in a few days, after I review this information and have a chance to speak with my boss about it?"

"Sure, I can call you back. How are you feeling about things?" Jeff shoots me a smile. Things are going great! Why don't I look more enthused?

His prospect is still chatting away. "As I mentioned last week," says Bob, "you guys are the solution we need right now. It's just a matter of time until we get budget for this, and my boss really wants to make it happen. I'll know more in a couple days, so let's talk then."

"How's Thursday at 10:00 a.m.?"

"Perfect. Send me a meeting maker on Outlook."

"Okay, Bob. We'll talk Thursday."

Jeff looks over at me with a big grin and says, "See? I told you I was on the right track with Bob!"

"Maybe," I say. "But are you convinced he can close the deal? What makes you think you're talking with the right person at this company?"

Jeff frowns, suddenly unsure. "He made an appointment with me, didn't he?"

NAVIGATING YOUR WAY TO A REAL DEAL

According to CSO Insights' 2008 Sales Performance Optimization Report, they surveyed more than 1,500 sales organizations, their reps

close 48.7 percent—almost half—of the deals in their pipeline forecasts. They lose 30.1 percent of the deals, and 21.2 percent of deals
end up a "no decision." What happened? When a deal is lost because
of "no decision," it's usually because the salesperson has aligned him-
or herself with the wrong person. The solution to this common problem is an often overlooked but vital skill: navigating.

Navigating is one of my favorite skills to coach, and one of the
most revealing. According to CSO Insights' 2008 Sales Performance
Optimization Report, most reps rarely admit they need to work on
this skill, because it deals with gatekeepers—and they believe that talking to gatekeepers and getting past them is a no-brainer: you either
have access to get in, or you get shut out. But very often, sales reps
mistake a high-level gatekeeper for someone who has real power.

Those people who are so happy to talk to you and promise everything are what I call *No-Po's*: people with *no power* to close the deal.
They are only there to waste your time and keep you from connecting
with the power buyer.

It's easy to surrender to the No-Po's offer of false hope because,
after dialing hundreds of calls, you've finally found someone who's
actually happy to talk to you! The hardest part is admitting to yourself that you've wasted time on a No-Po. But once you do, you can
finally start making headway in an organization. With skillful navigating, you can learn to quickly separate the No-Po's from the power
buyers and narrow down your prospects to the people who can make
the deal happen. All it takes is a little digging.

Navigating Basics

Navigating is a skill that requires courage, determination, curiosity,
and speed. I always like to compare it to what that television detective
Columbo used to do. His method of gathering information was to
ask lots of questions and stay just under the radar with a friendly,
nonthreatening approach. Once he had all the pieces, he was able to
put the puzzle together and solve the mystery. That is the navigation
skill.

When you approach information gathering in the right way, people (mostly No-Po's) can give you a lot of material without even realizing it. When you approach them the wrong way, however, you are noticed, discovered, and ultimately shut out.

Navigating is a unique skill because you are really not "selling"; you are just gathering and collecting valuable information that you will access as you continue your qualification and presentation efforts. So, basically, you are laying the foundation for a relationship when you are navigating.

Navigating Essentials

Here are some simple navigating techniques that will allow you to access information you never thought possible:

> Make sure the person you are looking for is still with the company. You don't want to leave a voice mail message for someone who is no longer part of the organization but has negotiated to keep a voice mail box active.

> Ask for help: "I wonder if you can help me." Remember, you are not selling your product or service.

> Your goal is to get a live voice. If you land in someone's voice mail, press the 0 or # keys to get out.

> Make your actions seamless and move quickly.

> Ask direct questions that will provide you with informative answers.

> Give information in order to receive it.

> Be confident, professional, and polite. Show respect and make your gatekeeper feel important.

> Be friendly and brief, and sound warm. Remember to give "verbal hugs."

> Identify yourself fully.

> Build rapport and camaraderie.

> Be persistent, tenacious, and enthusiastic.

> Don't leave tracks—no voice mails!

UNDERSTANDING HOW POWER WORKS
IN A SALES 2.0 ENVIRONMENT

The noisy, constantly moving Sales 2.0 landscape can hide real power and make No-Po's look like shining stars. A deep understanding of the nature of power in today's companies is basic to finding it. Fortunately, there are only three things you have to remember:

> Power is invisible.
>
> Power moves.
>
> Power hides.

Power Is Invisible

Does power reside at C-level, with the CEO, CFO, and all the other chiefs? Or does it reside with a person with the much more humble title "external management consultant," who may actually influence the budget? It's often hard to tell.

The explosion of impressive titles is a big part of the problem. Corporate culture is very status-conscious, and almost everybody *sounds* as though he or she might have power. Mergers and acquisitions create additional layers of management, new positions, new titles, and new roles and responsibilities. Add to this the fact that every organization doles out titles on its own terms, and you have a confusing mess. A director of marketing at one company, for example, might be a harried and powerless project manager, while an individual with the same title at a different company may have several million dollars at their disposal.

The key? Don't go after titles for their own sake. Find out where the power truly lies first.

Power Moves

Mergers, acquisitions, hiring and firing, corporate theft . . . the pace of business is now so fast that power relationships can shift in the course of a single sale. As companies merge and adopt Web 2.0 technology, the product and service offerings broaden—so a solution targeted at IT may now spill over to Marketing, Sales, Finance, and Operations.

Power Hides

The fast-moving Sales 2.0 gives power many organizational hiding places. The reasons fall into a general category I call "too many."

> ➤ **Too many names to choose from.** Popular software tools make it deceptively simple to find the names of people to talk to in a given organization. For example, if you search Apple using the Jigsaw precall search tool, you will find lots of potential contacts—883, to be precise. How are you supposed to know who, among these literally hundreds of people, is the one you want to contact? You have so many names to choose from that your chances of connecting with a No-Po—and getting strung along by false promises—are enormous.

> ➤ **Too many people involved in decision making.** According to the Executive Summary of Miller Heiman's 2008 Sales Best Practices Study, today's sales reps must persuade four to six more people for each sales opportunity they pursue. As the buying process becomes more complex and technical, procurement departments often consult IT or other areas of the business before making buying decisions. This brings more people into the process, and introduces more layers of management. More people are involved in making decisions—and fewer people with access to budgets.

> ➤ **Too many educated buyers.** Today's Internet-savvy customers are more informed and knowledgeable than ever. They can check out corporate websites and use search engines to compare solutions. As a result, you may find yourself engaged in long, technical discussions with people who can't qualify the sale. In fact, a prospect with *too much* technical knowledge may be a red flag for ferreting out a No-Po: it's usually the decision maker with the broader view who has the money to buy.

> **Too many distractions.** Once upon a time, before the Internet, desktop distractions consisted of a few wind-up toys. As we saw in Chapter 1, information overload has made productivity one of the biggest challenges for sales reps. But you're not the only one suffering. Desktop distractions also leave decision makers with less time to carefully consider your solution and make the appropriate decision.

STAY OUT OF THE NO-PO ZONE!

All of this noise and confusion predisposes decision makers to view you as just another distraction and your product as a faceless commodity. Their solution is to protect themselves with an army of gatekeepers dedicated to keeping you out. Your challenge is to get to them without being sidetracked by a No-Po. But it's surprisingly easy to get caught.

As inside sales reps, we are all fighting against time to capture and sustain attention and arouse curiosity. After we've dialed a hundred outbound calls in a week, with little success, we just want to connect with someone live. It's comforting to find someone who understands us, and who wants to talk. Because No-Po's *love* talking with vendors, they discourage you from talking with anyone else—especially their bosses.

No-Po's win you over by being cooperative. They ask for information and materials. They become your ally. You establish a mutually supportive rapport, and you believe you are making progress. You believe they are going to push your information through, and you begin to feel like an insider with access to more information. Soon, you believe the sale is getting closer because they invite more people to your conference calls and your demos. You may even go so far as to forecast this prospect on your sales report, assuring your manager that you'll bring in the deal.

Watch out! You've just been sucked into the No-Po Zone.

Spotting a No-Po

It's easy to spot the entry-level No-Po's—these are the receptionists, coordinators, administrators, and department secretaries that most salespeople are born knowing how to navigate around. But the more insidious No-Po's are the ones who aren't so easy to spot.

Unlike the traditional gatekeepers, these No-Pos are very knowledgeable and are part of the committee or department. They often hold a prestigious title, such as manager, director, engineer, administrator, analyst, or C-level executive. But although they earn more than receptionists and executive assistants, they hold roughly the same level of power when it comes to making purchasing decisions.

And, of course, they love to talk, especially to you, and they are knowledgeable about your product. Talking with you gives them information, ammunition to build a case, and makes them feel important.

We all like referrals. If your No-Po refers you to more people, you may be fooled into believing that you are getting closer to finding someone in power. Unfortunately, they are part of the No-Po's powerless entourage that sits on nonexistent budgets. They like to bounce ideas around, share new and different information, make additional requests, and get so comfortable with you that they share their frustrations of not knowing what is going on.

No-Po's are also very territorial. Because they have so little power in their own company, they're likely to take as much power as they can get from you, the outsider. If they admit that they need your service, it might confirm to their managers that they're deficient. As a result, they're threatened by you. And they never ever want you to talk to their boss, because that would give the whole show away.

Ten Red Flags for Identifying No-Po's

Once you learn to identify these ten bright-red flags, you'll probably be surprised at how many you've seen waving already—and ignored, because the person was so much fun to talk to:

1. *They say no right away,* before they've taken time to understand what your solution offers—because, essentially, they have no power to say yes.

2. *They love talking with you,* and act as if they have a lot of power.

3. *They ask you for more research,* demos, and competitive analyses, which creates a lot of busywork for you to do.

4. *They ask lots of questions*, and, while most of them are really good questions, they also require additional legwork on your part.

5. *They really like your product or service*, and they say they know *exactly* how it fits in and how they would implement it.

6. *They insist that you only speak with them* and discourage any contact with their boss.

7. *They assure you that they are your main contact.*

8. *They claim they have everything under control.*

9. *They schedule meetings that get rescheduled at the last minute* because something beyond their control and more important took priority.

10. *They stall* and ask you to call back next quarter.

NAVIGATING NO-PO'S USING THE 2x2 ORG CHART RULE

It's amazing how many salespeople stick with the same contact at a company. Most often that contact is the No-Po. It is important to call deeper and wider into the company, and building an org chart using the 2x2 org rule is the best way to do it.

Here's how it works: when you are gathering names, you map out the hierarchy, so you call two people up, down, across, each time you are prospecting into an organization. This will give you up to eight contacts.

Follow these five steps:

1. *Use your precall research tools to collect names.* For example, you look up a company and notice there are eighty-three people in the IT department. You start building your org chart by mapping these titles in a hierarchy. From highest to lowest, you may find the CTO, VP of IT, Director of IT, IT Manager, IT Administrator, and IT Coordinator. As you continue to build your org chart across, you may get names of people in the Marketing Department.

2. *Map all of these names on an org chart.* Start informally building an org chart, and put some names together as though you are build-

ing a giant jigsaw puzzle. Build titles from highest to lowest and start arranging them from the top down. For example, C-level titles such as CEO, CFO, and CTO will be at the top, with VP levels such as VP of IT, VP of Sales, and so on at the next level. What follows will be your Director level, under which will be the Manager level, under which will be the Administrator level, and so on. You can start by mapping it intuitively and then make calls to confirm the power structure.

3. *Cross-reference these names and titles into your contact management tool.* Your Salesforce automation tool is loaded with information, and it never hurts to look up the company to see if there has been previous activity in the past with someone from that company. These are usually the best people to call on, because a rapport with your company already exists.

4. *Determine whom to call first.* This is a significant decision, but not one to spend too much time on. Are you going to start low, or are you going to start high and go straight to the top? Generally, I suggest calling executive assistants when you are navigating. We will talk more about this important skill in Chapter 6, "Linking."

5. *Set a goal to reach at least six to eight contacts.* Work quickly, and keep calling to get a live contact.

SNIFFING OUT A NO-PO

No-Po's fear commitment and usually the types of responses you receive to various questions will confirm you are in No-Po land. Listen carefully and pay attention to the responses of your contact:

1. Always start by asking them how long they've been working in their position. Usually, if they haven't been there that long, they have little influence and budget allocation.

2. Ask lots of questions about the decision-making process. No-Po's will usually not name anyone in particular in their response, and everything points back to them. A typical vague response may sound like:

Our department oversees this and I'm working closely with all the individuals, so I'm your best contact.

3. The last thing you want to ask a No-Po is for their boss's name, because this may be the type of response you'll receive:

   I don't think it's necessary to be contacting my boss. He is pretty busy and besides, he'll just direct you back to me, so I'm the best person to speak with.

4. Check for cooperation with your questions and listen for vague responses. Here is an example of a classic vague response:

   There are a number of transformation efforts that are underway and one of our primary initiatives is this implementation. This means we will shift our resources to support how we work today. There is a lot of stabilization of the operations going on and getting that system implemented and supporting that will be our top priority. From that, there is certainly work we are trying to do to improve the skill sets around our ability to translate some of these customer contacts into a sales order or a lead at a minimum.

5. Ask questions to help you determine if your contact has been involved in both influencing and allocating budgets on large purchase decisions. If their response is vague, you can tell immediately they will not be involved:

   Budget is tight right now and in the past we could get this signed off. Now we must show a strong ROI in order to get something approved.

Inside Sales Insights: Recognizing a No-Po's E-Mail

No-Po's can be so nice on the phone that you willfully ignore the red flags. In e-mails, however, you may be able to spot them more easily. Here are some real examples that may look familiar.

```
Emily,
We just returned from our sales kickoff and, once
the dust settles, I would like to present your pro-
posal to the team. We had DDI provide us with great
```

sales training at the kickoff. Heard of them? If you can provide me with a side-by-side comparison, that will be helpful when I present your offerings to the team. I'll be in the office the rest of this week if you would like to discuss.

Thanks,
Mario

No-Po Red Flag: This e-mail is a brush-off. Mario has another provider. But if he can be convinced, he may be open to supporting your offerings. The fact that he is "presenting to a team" puts him in an information-gathering and researching position, which never carries much influence.

Hi Ben—

One more question for you. You're scheduled to deliver your Time Management module on the 15th, right? Regardless of the topic, I'd like to see if I can get down to Cupertino to observe your workshop. Would that be alright?

Thanks,
Sharon

No-Po Red Flag: Who has time to sit through and observe an entire workshop? This must mean she either wants to learn new skills or steal some ideas, or to convince herself that she has something better and won't need your services.

Hi Stephen,

Unfortunately, we were recently informed that what training budget we had was lost on 1 April with the start of FY09.

I think the information you provide is extremely relevant and I'll continue to forward it to my team. However, at this time, we don't have the budget to go forward with any type of official sales training.

I appreciate your follow-up and please stay in touch with me as Lauren Miceli is traveling and I'm your best contact.

Thanks!
Fran

No-Po Red Flag: Fran is just keeping you away and protecting her turf by discouraging any contact with anyone else. This may show uncertainty about her own power, too.

Hi Oscar,

Just a quick update for you. I did not want you to think I was ignoring you.

The department just went through a massive reorganization in Council Bluffs. Job descriptions are still being written and people are still being shuffled. This is going to take at least two to three months to settle.

Unfortunately we need to put this on hold until June/July before we can reasonably make another approach and bring it to the forefront of people's minds.

Thank you again,
Carl

No-Po Red Flag: Carl is reacting to situations beyond his control. He's projecting the negative fallout because he's uncertain about his power and his future.

WHY WE LOVE OUR NO-PO'S

No-Po's are endearing and salespeople are loyal. Some believe that after they have spent months with a No-Po, they may be "owed" the business. Others may truly believe they are helping the No-Po convince their boss to buy. They've formed a relationship with the No-Po and refuse to believe they have been wasting their time.

Salespeople get hired because of their ability to rebound from rejection and maintain a positive disposition. We are an ambitious and hopeful group, and we tend to listen with what I call "happy ears." We've got high quota pressure and management pressure to make our numbers, so it's inevitable that we listen for what we wish for. It's typical for ambitious and motivated salespeople to believe and hope that something positive will happen.

If something about this situation strikes you as familiar, I'm not surprised. It's a lot like dating a person who seems to love you, who'll do everything for you, who promises you the moon . . . but in reality, they're unavailable. They're not right for you, and they're never going to commit to you. Everyone sees it but you. Your friends and family discourage you from being with that person. But you hold onto the hope they will change, and believe they will, only to feel betrayed when, inevitably, the relationship falls apart.

Seven Reasons Why We Keep Hanging On to Our No-Pos

1. We want to believe something will really happen and listen with "happy ears."

2. We believe we can convince them when we think things are getting closer.

3. We are motivated when we see small changes and believe things are moving along.

4. We want to help them turn things around.

5. We think we are moving in the right direction but our ego will not admit we are not.

6. We have a sense of entitlement and believe they owe us for all the work we've done on the sale.

7. They like us so we assume they are cooperating and will give us the business.

WHEN YOU'VE STUCK WITH A NO-PO TOO LONG

There's nothing wrong in engaging with No-Po—at the right time, and for the right reasons. They can act as a coach or an ally, and be a great technical and business informant. Engaging with them on your own terms, and with the knowledge that they are there to direct you to the power buyer, is a great strategy. But feeling that you're stuck with them, and not knowing how to disengage, is something else entirely.

Even after we realize we've mistaken a No-Po for a power buyer, it can be hard to let go. We don't want to go around them—we know them too well. Anyway, they won't give us their boss's name. And, let's be honest—we don't want to pull them off our forecast and have to admit it was because of something as simple as we talked with the wrong person.

Most reps have to hit rock bottom before they're ready to let go. Reality hits when they realize they've been stuck on a deal because they truly believed their No-Po would actually make something happen. The No-Po told them to stay away from calling around them and above them, and they listened. So they have no other contacts at the company. Meanwhile, the salesperson's forecast has suffered because they haven't closed the sale.

WHEN THE NO-PO MUST PROTECT HIS OR HER TURF

No-Po's usually lack power or they are uncertain of the degree of power they actually have. The last thing they want is for you to show them up. They become very territorial and adamant that you not contact their boss. Because they lack power, exercising control over vendors gives them a false sense of that power. They will complain about having too many initiatives on their plate, but will assert that they have it all under control, and will continue to string you along with false promises.

WATCH OUT FOR THE NO-PO ENTOURAGE

You might think that because more people are getting involved along the way that you are getting closer to a deal. Wrong! Beware of the No-Po entourage. That's right, these are more powerless decision makers who take lengthy meetings with vendors and ask for more information so they can become more knowledgeable in their jobs. We get sucked in with them because we think that gathering more names means we are getting closer, we are always encouraged to ask for referrals, and we simply can't refuse scheduling an appointment with so many interested people.

SAYING GOODBYE TO NO-PO'S

The thought of risking the loyal relationship with your No-Po can be daunting. But once you realize you have nothing to lose—and everything to gain—it's worth considering. It's also worth doing right. Don't burn bridges. In the fast-moving Sales 2.0 world, today's No-Po may turn out to be tomorrow's power buyer.

Still, it probably won't be easy. Garth Moulton, co-founder of Jigsaw, an e-mail marketing company, wrote this in response to one of my blogs about No-Po's: "I just wanted to let you know that your last blog post is spot on and probably the biggest challenge for our Idaho team. They are collectively such a nice group of people it is very hard for them to let go of the No-Po's!!!!!"

Getting around your No-Pos effectively requires careful preparation and proper messaging. Above all, you don't want to just go over their heads with no warning, or in an abrupt or rude way, because that will almost certainly come back to bite you some day. This means not leaving voice mails or e-mails for the new prospect that can be forwarded back down to your No-Po. Be polite, thoughtful, and have the confidence to go after the person who can actually help you.

The following seven steps will help you let your No-Po down gently but firmly so you can both move on:

1. *Be nice, but be firm.* Make sure you continue to assure the No-Po of your loyalty, while also setting expectations about having access to a higher level. This will set the stage for leaving.

2. *Document what you've learned.* Gather all the knowledge you've accumulated from the No-Po about their business needs, challenges, technical environment, competition, culture, and so on. You will need all this to effectively integrate into your conversations with more people.

3. *Begin to navigate.* Start collecting more names of possible prospects in the organization. Build an org chart to understand where they sit in the hierarchy, as described earlier in this chapter.

4. *Call inside the organization.* Gather and confirm information. Get people live—do not leave tracks by leaving voice mail or e-mail!

5. *Stop calling the No-Po.* Resist any temptations you have to contact your No-Po just because it's comfortable, you have history, they're cooperative, and you believe they owe you something.

6. *Practice detachment.* Reduce the forecast probability of this prospect closing. No expectations or assumptions here.

7. *Believe in yourself.* Believe you are no longer a groveling salesperson but a consultant who has every right to their business. Believe in the value you and your solution bring. Don't despair or beat yourself up for sticking with a No-Po. The sooner you figure things out and move on, the better off you will be.

GOING AROUND YOUR NO-PO TO ADDRESS THE POWER BUYER

First, make sure you've said goodbye to your No-Po. Then prepare your call to the power buyer.

Position yourself as a solution specialist, a consultant—and not a desperate salesperson who needs to hit your quota this month. Believe in yourself: you have something of value to say to this higher-level decision maker. Before you make contact, review the following ten steps:

1. Deliver your introduction and immediately name the person you've been working with—your No-Po.

2. State the valid business reason for your call.

3. Reveal how much you know about the person you're speaking with.

4. Verify and confirm their business needs.

5. Inquire about their familiarity with your company.

6. Confirm executive approval of project, budget, and timeline.

7. Discuss goals, objectives, and expectations.

8. Gain confirmation on the sequence of events.

9. Confirm their chain of command; get escorted down.

10. Gain their commitment to stay in the loop.

You want to get the person on the phone live. Don't leave a trail of e-mail or phone messages that can come back to haunt you. Here's a sample scenario and conversation to show you how this works in real life:

Sample Scenario: For the past several months, you've been talking with a No-Po: Dan Ryan, the manager of IT for a medium-sized software company. You've done some navigating, and discovered that the person with the budget to buy is Scott Wood, director of IT.

The phone call: You gather your notes together—you write down everything you learned while navigating the company—and make the call. You know it's important to get Scott live, not leave a message with his secretary or send him an e-mail. It takes twenty attempts, but it finally happens.

"Hi Scott, glad I caught you. I'll be brief. I'm Sue Smith with JenCo, and I've been working closely with Dan Ryan from your IT team for the past few months.

[Pause, and listen for signs of recognition and acknowledgment or no recognition.]

"Great. I understand some of your current initiatives since your recent merger. In the last three months, you recently implemented *[mention three things you've learned about the company from his perspective that relate to your product or service]* and I'm curious to learn more about your short-term goals and expectations."

[Verify and confirm understanding and direction.]

"I would also like to make myself available to you as a resource and solutions provider in this area because my expertise is in . . ." *[sell your credentials based on your solution and his needs].*

"Will you be making decisions on this front and allocating budget to Dan, or is there someone else I can also be in contact with? Thanks, I'll continue to work with Dan Ryan, and I'll also contact Mark Atobe based on your suggestion. I certainly will keep you in the loop. I appreciate your generous time on the phone today."

─────────────── The Power Reality Check ───────────────

Having trouble letting go? Here are some typical real-life scenarios from perfectly reasonable reps who've been fooled by No-Pos. Run these power reality checks on yourself when you think you may have given your loyalty to a No-Po.

Hopelessly Romantic Ron: *"I've been working this big deal for many months, and received renewed hope last month when a new IT manager stepped in to replace the old one. Things are moving much faster with this new manager—he's already familiar with the product line from a previous company he worked at. In our last call, he even articulated an implementation strategy and said we will talk after he closes out this quarter. This is a no-brainer because he loves our solution, knows how to deploy it, and they definitely need us."*

Reality Check: The red flag here is waving right in Ron's face: the person is new to the company and hasn't earned enough influence yet. It's great that the IT manager is familiar with the solution from his previous company, but Ron needs to find out if this manager was part of the decision to bring his product in when he was at his last company, or if he was just an end-user. Before this manager came on board, how did Ron leverage his influence with other decision makers?

When things move faster in the sales process, it's easy to assume it's moving in the right direction. However, just talking about an implementation solution isn't enough. How has the new IT manager articulated an implementation strategy? Is it high-level or more technical? Where will he get funding for this product?

Sociable Sally: *"I've been calling on this huge company, and I'm certain I am aligned with the right person. I had my doubts about my contact at first, but she's done so much and really wants to bring my services in. She's introduced me to more people, and held a conference call with four people from her department. She coordinated the meeting and was very vocal about how much our services are needed."*

Reality Check: Don't be fooled into believing you are getting closer to closing the sale just because more people are involved. You may have encountered the powerless entourage. They are part of the powerless royalty who sit around and wonder who has the budget. The good news is that you have more people involved, but the bad news could be that they all lack power.

Friendly Fred: *"I'm good friends with my contact—they definitely want us in there. He's frustrated, though, because things are a mess in his area. Yeah, he confides in me and tells me everything—even forwards internal announcements. I have an advantage, right? I'm getting the purchase order ready because I know he'll pull the trigger soon."*

Reality Check: *When we're good friends with our contact, we may assume certain things because of that friendship. If the contact is frustrated, he may have negative power. So don't be surprised if he cashes in on his friendship and calls you next month asking for a job!*

NAVIGATING STRATEGIES

1. Remember: Power is invisible, power moves, and power hides. The Sales 2.0 landscape makes it harder than ever to find the power. Never assume you know who has the power in an organization.

2. Pay attention to No-Po red flags. When your deal has failed to move for far too long and you never get to speak to the boss, you're probably wasting your time with a No-Po. Look for red flags and phone and e-mail clues and take a reality check.

3. Navigate the organization to separate the No-Po's from the power buyers. Use your phone skills to elicit information about who really makes the decisions and who controls the budget. Document everything.

4. Learn to quickly "sniff out" a No-Po. Listen for vague responses to your questions and look for signs of their protecting their turf.

5. Let your No-Po down gently—never burn bridges. You must let go of the No-Po before moving on, but do keep that person as an ally. Remember: power travels!

6. Prepare a calling strategy for your power player. Do careful research concerning the needs and challenges they may face.

7. Call the power buyer. Have a business conversation that positions you as the expert consultant.

8. Review, refresh, and revise your forecast. If you discover you've pinned your hopes on a No-Po, remove that prospect from your forecast now. If you connect with a power player, revise your forecast upward. Be honest. Don't set yourself up to fail.

9. Never stop navigating! Power is always on the move, and you always want to know where it is.

CHAPTER 4

Questioning
Building Trust, One Question at a Time

Don't spend so much time trying to choose the perfect opportunity,
that you miss the right opportunity.

—Michael Dell

In this chapter, you'll get valuable insight into:

- ⊘ Whether your own questioning style creates comfort and trust
- ⊘ Whether your questions are relevant, insightful, and make people think
- ⊘ Why you may lack the courage to continue in the needs discovery process, choosing instead to rush the call and end your hope of selling something

You'll learn tools and tactics to help you:

- ⊘ Understand the order, strategy, style, formulation, and criteria of effective questioning
- ⊘ Differentiate between telling and selling
- ⊘ Organize your questions using established qualification criteria
- ⊘ Learn analytical questioning skills and focus on formulating questions that get the answers you need

When I stepped into Rick's cubicle, he got right to the point. "I hope you're going to tell me what to do with all these lousy leads," he said with a grim smile.

"What happened to all the new leads you received for your call campaign?"

"That was a bad list, those leads were a joke. I could use more high-level leads though."

"What's happening?" I asked. *"Why aren't any of these leads you are calling on converting into opportunities or appointments? Do you mind if I sit in on some of your calls and listen to your qualification efforts?"*

"Sure," replied Rick. *"I was just about to make one. Listen in!"* He started punching in the numbers.

"Hi, this is Rick Reynolds. Oh, did I catch you at a bad time? . . . I'm calling to follow up on the recent webinar you attended . . . Are you guys having any problems I can help you with? . . . I see. Do you make the decisions on these solutions? . . . Okay, is this a budgeted project? . . . Will this project happen within the next three to six months? . . . Do you have any more questions for me?"

Rick hung up, shaking his head.

"Well," I said, *"what did you think of this call?"*

"I told you," he said, shrugging his shoulders. *"These are pretty useless leads."*

"Rick, it's not the quality of your leads that is the problem. It's the quality of your questions."

QUESTIONING UNCOVERS NEEDS, QUALIFIES LEADS, CONTROLS CALLS

According to an IDC report, 80 percent of marketing expenditures on lead generation is wasted because the leads are ignored by salespeople. Yet, according to CSO Insights' 2008 "Improve Lead Generation and Clean Up Your Pipeline" white paper, there's a big disconnect between sales and marketing on the definition of a "qualified lead." In addition, the paper concludes by observing that when companies aren't aligned, there's a huge tax: 10 percent on closing opportunities and 5.7 percent on revenues. Nonetheless, companies pressure reps to quickly qualify leads, and to continue to dump more leads into the sales bucket. But when marketing and sales don't agree on what constitutes a qualified lead, it's easy for reps to chase the wrong leads or scream at marketing for more leads to add to their bucket. The kicker is, in inside sales you are only as good as your last lead, and there is a direct link between exceeding quotas and having stronger leads. Why, then, are salespeople still chasing business they don't want?

Questioning is your first chance to get inside a company and look around. Your questions act as your eyes on every phone call. Questioning is still a skill that is best accomplished by phone and not via e-mail, and technique is critical to uncovering customer needs and opportunities. Strong questioning skills can immediately capture control of the call and lead a sale to close. Poor questioning skills can sink even the best leads in a matter of minutes.

Today's prospects have lost patience with vendors. They are tired of the same questions and annoyed with outdated sales tactics. Too often, unskilled or poorly trained reps ask too few questions, waste too much time asking meaningless questions of the wrong people, or put prospects in a headlock with a barrage of questions that sounds like an interrogation.

Developing the important skill of questioning requires you to examine your qualification efforts from the inside out. How does your questioning style create comfort and trust? Do your questions sound relevant and insightful, or do your prospects feel as though they are being interrogated with rapid-fire questioning? Why do people really like talking with you? Is it because your questions make them think? How do you get the courage to ask one more question and boldly move through your qualifying efforts? Does your curious mind lead you toward learning and absorbing more? Questioning entails tremendous risk. It takes courage and instinct. Fortunately, a strong questioning technique is a skill that you can learn and put to use right away.

SALES 2.0 IS ABOUT SUBSTANCE

Surviving in today's selling battlefield requires you to establish substantial relationships. Today's buyers are more informed than they used to be, but they are also more confused and fearful. When everything is uncertain and unstable, and budgets are under scrutiny, salespeople must approach their qualification efforts with more curiosity, depth, and substance than just the old "Got a project?" question—especially when only a small percentage of leads that are generated are likely to be "sales ready." During tough economic times, salespeople must take the time to strengthen current relationships, rekindle past relationships, and plant seeds for the future.

Skillful questioning habits build rapport and trust. If you ask good questions and listen to the responses to hear your prospects' needs, you will guide them straight to their comfort zone, hold the focus through all their confusion, and very likely close a sale.

It's important to do your homework. Today's buyers are demanding that sales reps know who they are before the call. As with good introducing skills, you must come in with a certain level of knowledge about the target organization. This starts before you make the call, with the use of all those great Sales 2.0 research tools at your command.

Finely honed hunting skills are becoming a lost art, because so many inside salespeople believe they can be replaced with automation tools and e-mail exchanges. These tools serve a purpose: they can help you to determine your qualification strategy based on the source of the lead by tracking your prospect's interest through website visits, webinar attendance, white paper downloads, or identifying which list they are calling from. You can research your target organization and perhaps learn about the company's direction, new product releases, position in the market, and size of the various departments and teams. Bringing all this data to a call helps jump-start qualification efforts and increases the chances of having a meaningful conversation and getting results.

But here's the real point: With so many marketing automation vendors bringing products to help with lead generation, cultivation, and management, there is a greater need for the high-touch aspect of effective questioning and listening skills. These critical skills cannot be managed online because they require a dynamic dialogue, a conversation, a discussion—a direct human interchange best served by the immediacy of live voices over the phone. Think about it: Will a busy prospect really want to spend time responding to a long e-mail string filled with qualification questions they must answer?

What Customers Hate About You

In Kelley Robertson's 2008 book, *The Secrets of Power Selling,* he found eighty reasons why customers dislike salespeople. The top seven are highlighted as "What Customers Hate About You":

1. Not listening (addressed in Chapter 5, "Listening")

2. Talking too much (addressed in this chapter)

3. Lack of knowledge (addressed in this chapter)

4. Lack of follow-up (addressed in Chapter 9, "Closing")

5. Lying (addressed in Chapter 8, "Handling Objections")

6. Failing to understand their needs (addressed in this chapter)

7. Refusal to take "no" for an answer (addressed in Chapter 8, "Handling Objections")

QUALITY VERSUS QUANTITY: WHAT'S THE DIFFERENCE?

According to CSO Insights' 2008 "Improve Lead Generation and Clean Up Your Pipeline" findings, when revenue and quota attainment increase in direct relationship to a salesperson's ability to qualify and prioritize leads, it is essential to be able to distinguish quality from quantity. And in order to understand the difference, you must first understand the difference between qualification and questioning.

When you receive a lead, you first *qualify* it to determine if it is a viable opportunity you want to chase: one that is aligned to your "sweet spot," and a potential match between your offerings and your prospect's requirements. Once you determine that the lead is qualified, you can ask *questions* that help you develop these leads into opportunities. In Sales 2.0, the sales and marketing departments usually work together. Marketing will qualify opportunities by creating demand generation and nurturing leads, and sales will chase them.

Marketing generates leads through such methods as webinars, trade shows, direct mail campaigns, white papers, presentations, demos, and trial evaluations, and sales teams follow up with preliminary qualification efforts. Many inside sales organizations are structured with lead development, qualification, and generation teams that may report to marketing. The lead development teams ask questions on a tactical level to uncover needs, identify current challenges, develop interest, and build trust. This is a metrics-driven activity—conversion rates and cost per lead are the buzzwords. So the focus is mostly on quantity, and the qualification efforts are usually pretty narrow, such as qualifying based on a prospect's budget and timeframe.

If budget and timeframe fall within three to six months, marketing turns the lead over to inside sales, telesales, and direct sales teams that report to the sales organization. These teams then spend time cultivating the lead and diving deeper into the needs discovery and relationship-building part of the process.

The inside sales rep is expected to move the lead to a strategic level, creating urgency, qualifying value, establishing competitive differentiation, and building trust and loyalty.

YOU CAN NO LONGER AFFORD TO WASTE A CALL

In today's tough economic times, salespeople must work smarter. When they spend 33 percent of their time finding the right people, they must maximize and salvage each call with stronger questioning efforts. They can't afford to skip the qualification process, or do half the job. The lead nurturing process requires attention and definition.

Working very hard at chasing the wrong business is a waste of your time. Believing you are moving it forward by volunteering white papers, demos, proposals, competitive analyses, and even on-site troubleshooting as a way to qualify prospects will not work. Chasing everything that looks like an opportunity keeps you busy, but ineffective. You're working harder, but not smarter. Begging for discounts with low-margin customers is unacceptable, and adding more leads isn't the answer.

Learning the art of questioning, and putting it into practice, will get you there. Formulating questions with a definite strategy will allow you to hold your weight on sales calls.

THE FOUR COMPONENTS OF QUESTIONING

It's a simple equation: The more you bring to the call, the more you will get out of it.

As you've already learned, low connect rates are common when making outbound introductory calls. When you finally *do* have a live call, it's important to get the most from it. If you have earned extra seconds because your introduction aroused interest, then you can launch into your questions with confidence:

1. Your *strategy or plan* will capture control of the call and determine how well you have qualified your opportunity and established trust.

2. How you *formulate* your questions will create the dialogue in your relationship.

3. The *style* in which you ask your questions will intrigue the prospect and encourage bigger responses.

4. The *order* in which you ask will provide a deeper needs discovery and open the door to their world.

The art of questioning requires you to master each of these components, and to choreograph them in each call you make.

STRATEGY AND PLANNING: THE SMART SELLING QUALIFICATION CRITERIA

"So, what's your budget over the next twelve months? How about your timeframe for new projects?" Could these questions be any more vague? Can asking them actually get you any closer to understanding a prospect's needs? In today's uncertain economic climate, prospects have absolutely no idea what their budget and their timeframe should be! If you keep asking the same vague, pointless questions, you'll get the same vague response. Or just a hang-up. Calling without a plan is the fastest way to get nowhere. Face it: If you don't know where you want to go, you'll always end up spinning your wheels. Having a questioning strategy in place before you begin gives you a map you can follow to your desired destination: a sale.

When criteria for a qualified lead aren't well established, it's easy to let go of the right deal without even knowing it. Agreeing on B.A.N.T. (Budget, Authority, Need, and Timeline) isn't enough. My Smart Selling qualification criteria create a proven—and winning—questioning plan that generates qualified leads. They encompass eight distinct qualification categories for you to capture on each lead, and reconfirm at every link in the decision-making chain:

1. Current environment
2. Business need
3. Decision-making process
4. Decision-making criteria
5. Competition
6. Timeframe
7. Budget
8. Next steps

Make sure you understand this order and touch on each of these important categories during your qualification efforts. Don't wait for your second or third or fourth call to get to all these categories. Be ambitious with your qualification efforts. Let's take a closer look at what each category entails.

Current Environment

The prospect's current (technical) environment is a snapshot of their internal world. It's the safest category to ask about (which is why it's first) because it invites the prospect to speak about themselves and helps you determine if they are worth spending time on.

The prospect's current technical environment includes what they have installed, how many users they have, and which platforms they are running on. Be careful to spend only as much time as you need to on this category. It's common for salespeople to get entangled in extremely lengthy discussion with No-Po's who love to talk and talk about their current technical environment, but are not capable of having a business discussion because they are not the business decision maker you really need to reach!

Sample questions:
- ➤ "What is your current network infrastructure?"
- ➤ "How are you currently set up?"
- ➤ "What type of platform are you running on?"
- ➤ "What applications are you using on the network?"

Business Need

Once you've uncovered information about your prospect's current environment, this may enable you to predict their needs and challenges. If you decide they may be worth spending more time on, you will want to determine whether you can meet their needs. Your questioning here digs for compelling business issues or events driving their organization to take action. What is truly motivating your prospect to buy? This helps you to uncover the prospect's pain—what is broken and causing them to be unproductive and what is the business impact of that challenge—and alerts you to what you might be able to help them with. (Chapter 5, "Listening," describes the important issue of pain in depth.)

Sample questions:
- ➤ "What issues are you facing right now?"
- ➤ "In what way can you improve what you currently have?"
- ➤ "What type of growing pains are you experiencing?"
- ➤ "How is the performance? Any bottlenecks?"
- ➤ "How will implementing a new solution impact your ability to serve your customers?"

> "What is your business objective or initiative?"
> "What are your priorities in improving these?"

Decision-Making Process

There's no excuse for not knowing with whom you are speaking. As we discussed in Chapter 3, "Navigating," it is essential to establish who your contact is early in the qualification process, and to determine the decision-making structure. This is where you do it. You will need to discover who the decision makers are in the organization, and their level of involvement and influence.

Sample questions:
> "Can you walk me through your decision-making process?"
> "What is your role in the decision-making process?"
> "What other groups get involved in the decision-making process?"
> "What is the decision-making process, from the validation to the approval phase?"
> "Who will make the . . . economic decision (who has final sign-off/ veto power)? Technical decision (comparing speeds and feeds)? User decision (departments impacted)?"

Decision-Making Criteria

Once you've uncovered information about the prospect's current environment, business needs, and decision-making process, you can focus on your prospect's decision-making criteria. The answers to your questions will not only benefit you, but will help them articulate how they evaluate new solutions and what they base their evaluation on, as well as what they consider important or critical. Focus your questions on the criteria that have been established for the project.

Sample questions:
> "Can you help me understand your criteria for the ideal solution?"
> "What is most important to you in a good solution?"

> "What top three features do you look for when evaluating a solution?"

Competition

Even though the prospect may have explained their competitive landscape when you asked about their current environment, don't assume anything. Too many deals are lost because the salesperson failed to ask or was afraid to know the answer to this all-important question: *"What's my competition?"*

Asking about the competitive landscape is an essential category, because some level of competition always exists. Getting into the habit of asking this question will reduce any surprises along the way.

Sample questions:

> "Where are you in your research process?"
> "What other vendor solutions do you have in-house?"
> "What led you to look at these other vendors?"
> "What other solutions have you looked at?"

Timeframe

Sales happen when the timing is right, but timing is one of the hardest things to predict. Determining a timeframe requires a strong understanding of the prospect's business needs, their pains and requirements, how critical the pain is, and what power sources will be involved. Usually, when the pain is very high and you have connected with the power buyer, things happen a lot faster.

Remember that answers about timeframe and budget will always change, depending on to whom you are speaking and how urgent they see the need for your solution.

Sample questions:

> "Can you walk me through your timeline, from research to implementation?"

- ➤ "When would you like to be up and running?"
- ➤ "What is the compelling event or deadline on this project?"
- ➤ "What will happen between now and then to make this a better time for you?"

Budget

You've learned what your prospect has installed in their current environment, what they are challenged with, when they need to implement a solution, and who will pull the trigger. Now you are ready to ask the budget question. Ask questions to help you determine if there even is a budget, and how much they have allocated for this project.

Sample questions:
- ➤ "How does the budgeting process work within your organization?"
- ➤ "What kind of dollar amount has been allocated for this project?"
- ➤ "How much money has been approved for this project?"
- ➤ "What does your funding look like for new projects/solutions?"

Next Steps

Wait! Don't hang up until you have articulated the next steps. In Chapter 1, "Time Management," we talked about action steps you should articulate before hanging up from the call. You may want to go back and review these.

Remember that you want to move this sale forward. Before you leave this call, make sure that you and the prospect are on the same page by locking in some action steps.

Sample questions:
- ➤ "What happens now?"
- ➤ "Where do we go from here?"
- ➤ "What other departments would you recommend I contact?"

FORMULATING QUESTIONS

It's vital for salespeople to build an arsenal of good questions. When I listen in on great salespeople in action, I am always seduced by their questions. The way they formulate their questions is intriguing, and they clearly have their prospect under control. When I listen to the way they string their words together, I am impressed by their instinct in knowing which question to ask next and their genuine curiosity in learning what the prospect has to say. They capture important information from each call simply by the way they formulate their questions.

Let's say you want to find out about the technical infrastructure of the organization. Asking, *"How are you guys currently set up?"* will give you a completely different answer than asking, *"Can you please walk me through your technical environment to help me understand which are your dominant platforms and the number of users in each?"* The first question may lead to confusion about exactly what you're asking. The second question is specific, and actually helps the prospect provide the answer you need.

Here's another example, this time about the decision-making process. If you ask the question, *"Are you the decision maker on this project?"* a No-Po may actually say yes. A better question is this one: *"Can you share with me who usually gets involved in making decisions and how the committee comes together?"* The response may send you off in a new and more productive direction.

STYLE: IT'S HOW YOU ASK THE QUESTION

Substance is great, but style will help you uncover the core issues and understand more quickly. Making a phone call puts you right in the prospect's personal space. If your questions make them feel comfortable with you, you'll be halfway to a sale. But if your style makes them want to get away from you as quickly as possible, they will! We'll take a quick look at what *not* to do, and then get on to effective questioning styles.

Bad Questioning Styles

Asking questions—even the best questions—in the wrong way is the quickest road to a hang-up. Questioning that seems invasive can put the prospect off and creates distance. A robotic questioning voice discourages any hope that a relationship will form. When you're dialing forty outbound calls per day, sorting quickly through a bucket of potential leads, it's all too easy to make one or more of the following errors in questioning techniques—especially if you haven't done your homework on the prospect ahead of time.

Interrogative Style. *"Are you the person who makes the decisions on technology for your organization? Uh-huh. And I would like to know how many users you currently have in your company since last year. Uh-huh. And when you attended our last demo, what did you think? And are you familiar with our solution? Uh-huh. And would you be the person who creates budget for this product?"*

Help! I'm under attack! This rapid-fire questioning manner doesn't demonstrate any listening skills. If you never give the prospect a chance to talk, you're guaranteed not to learn anything. It's commonly used by reps who just want to hammer through a list of weak questions and move on to make more calls on their campaign.

Apologetic or Tentative Style. *"Um, I'm so sorry to bother you. This doesn't seem like a good time, does it? Well, I can call you back. No? The reason is because I wanted to ask you a few questions. Can I just ask a question now and we can reschedule this call for next week?"*

An apologetic questioning style puts you in a weak position and can invite more objections from the prospect. It's a common trap for salespeople who are new to the role or to the company, and who feel insecure about how to handle the answers they receive. This fear usually settles around asking the tough questions about competition and budget.

Volunteering-the-Answer Style. *"So it doesn't sound like this time you will get funding for this project. When you are looking at vendors, are you looking to work with more prestigious organizations so ours would be too* small for you?" "So this doesn't sound like a purchase you want to make this quarter—is it fair to assume this product is too robust for your needs?"

When reps fear rejection, they can easily create it themselves without realizing it by assuming a negative answer without bothering to confirm. They often sound very understanding, volunteering an easy out embedded in the question. Although we may believe in providing choices for our prospects, if we ask a question and volunteer to answer it at the same time, it doesn't allow for strong probing of needs.

Yes-or-No Style. *"Is this a . . . ?" "Do you . . . ?" "Will you . . . ?" "Are you . . . ?"*

This closed-ended style is not recommended on introductory calls when you want to delicately uncover needs. These questions do not lead to further productive conversation! You can only get one of two answers—yes or no—and it's especially risky on new calls.

Good Questioning Styles

Your goal with every call should always be to encourage, engage, and build trust and rapport. Try to follow the 70/30 rule: Ask questions 30 percent of the time, listen 70 percent of the time. A good questioning style is the way to ensure this will happen.

Ask Open-Ended Questions. This is a great way to gather new information, because open-ended questions encourage the prospect to talk in more depth. Vary your questioning methods, move away from the traditional "five W's," and ask questions that call for descriptive answers:

> - "Please tell me about . . ."
> - "Describe for me . . ."
> - "Walk me through . . ."

Ask Precision Questions. These reveal your customer's true needs and help you understand the issues. I love these questions, because they really dive under the surface, sharpening up the vague or fuzzy responses we tend to receive. Your precision question will always start with these formulations:

> ➤ "How specifically do you . . . ?"
> ➤ "What exactly is your goal . . . ?"

Echo Their Response in Your Question. Basically, you take what the prospect says and say it back to them in your own words. This is a great relationship-building technique that also helps you confirm that you are getting correct information. We'll go into this more deeply in the next chapter, "Listening." Start your questions like this:

> ➤ "If I understand you correctly . . . . ?"
> ➤ "What I hear you saying is . . ."

THE ORDER OF QUESTIONING: DOING THE QUESTIONING DANCE

The magic in a sales call really happens when the dialogue begins. Most of this is based not only on what questions to ask, how they are formulated, and how you ask them, but knowing *when* to ask them. Timing is everything when organizing your questions.

Here's a game I play with participants in my trainings. I invite you to give it a try. Do your best, and we'll revisit it at the end of this section. The following ten questions are sample questions you would ask on an outbound call and are out of order. Reorganize them in the way that you think will elicit the best answers from your prospect:

1. "What is driving your interest in our solution?"
2. "What information do you need to make your decision?"
3. "What type of budget do you have set aside for this project?"
4. "What types of platforms are you currently running on?"
5. "What is your timeline; when do you plan to purchase?"
6. "What is important to you in evaluating a vendor?"
7. "What stage are you at in your research process?"

8. "Are you familiar with our company?"
9. "What is your role in the decision-making process?"
10. "How is your current process working?"

Asking questions in the right order has a lot to do with instinct. I used to think this was a skill that could not be taught, but I've changed my mind. If you know the secret, you too can learn to do the questioning dance. Here's the key: ask the next question *based on the answer you just received.*

Doing the questioning dance means listening to the prospect's response and moving your next question in a direction that aligns with that response. If you ask your questions in the wrong order because you're nervous or inattentive or working off a script, the prospect doesn't think they are being heard. And they're not! All you've done is demonstrate that you are not listening or using your sales instincts.

Now that you know the key, take another look at the list of ten questions. If you want to reorder them again, go ahead. When you're ready, keep reading.

While there's no perfect order—because every live call is different—the following order of outbound questions will provide a stronger *path* to the needs discovery process. It will help you to establish a stronger rapport and cooperation with your prospect, as well as to control the call and ultimately the quality of the information you gather:

1. "Are you familiar with our company?"
2. "What types of platforms are you currently running on?"
3. "How is your current process working?"
4. "What is driving your interest in our solution?"
5. "What is your role in the decision-making process?"
6. "What information do you need to make your decision?"
7. "What stage are you at in your research process?"
8. "What is important to you in evaluating a vendor?"
9. "What is your timeline; when do you plan to purchase?"
10. "What type of budget do you have set aside for this project?"

Cubicle
Chronicles

──────────────── Questioning Reality Check ────────────────

The experiences of at least one of these inside sales warriors may resonate with your own. Read on for some coaching solutions.

Rapid Randy: Randy blows through leads too fast. He's always eager to qualify the call and tends to jump in with questions prematurely, especially about budget and timeframe. When the prospect shuts down, Randy wonders what happened.

Reality Check: Timing matters. It's important to plan the questions and to time them well, complementing client answers. Choose and formulate your questions wisely *during* the call as well as before-hand. Asking sensitive questions too early can distance your prospect. Instead, start by asking questions about their current environment to get them to talk and establish rapport, since this is a nonthreatening questioning category.

Closed-Ended Cleo: Cleo doesn't feel very creative about how she formulates her questions. She tends to get short answers that don't really go anywhere except to a dead end.

Reality Check: The manner in which you formulate your questions will have a direct impact on your answers. If we start our calls with too many closed-ended questions (*"Is this a good time to talk? "Are you familiar with our company?"*), we'll get a short response—either yes or no. Instead, organize your questions this way: open-ended, paraphrase, open-ended, paraphrase, precision, open-ended, closed, open-ended.

Presenting Paul: Paul gets so excited when someone expresses interest in his product/solution that he moves right into pitching mode—and loses them.

Reality Check: One of the toughest things for salespeople to do is to stop and listen after they ask a question—and this is also the best way for Paul to break his habit. It's only time to sell when you have a good understanding of your prospect's needs—which you can only uncover after asking the right questions and listening to the answers. Remember the 70/30 rule. Before Paul launches into pitch mode, he needs to double-check his qualification criteria and make sure he's asked all the relevant questions.

QUESTIONING STRATEGIES

1. Bring information in order to get information from each call. Utilize your sales tools and come in prepared to engage in a deeper and richer qualification process.

2. Remember that it's about quality, not quantity. Don't let metrics discourage you from diving in and learning about your prospect. If you let go of leads too soon, you'll miss out on some potential opportunities.

3. Have a questioning plan. Set your objectives before you make the call. Know exactly what you'll need in order to help the customer buy. Be prepared with additional questions, and know what ideas you want to develop as you compose your questions.

4. Be conversational. Good questions lead to dialogue and dialogue leads to closing. You should react to their answers, respond, and build on them. If your questions are survey-style, your prospects will feel as though they are being interrogated. Spend time listening to responses instead of thinking about what you are going to say next.

5. Don't use manipulative questions. Avoid high-pressure questions that give the impression you are "selling" the prospect. Remember that you want to *help* people buy—not force them to buy.

6. Be clear and concise. Ask the question only once. Don't accept fuzzy words and phrases; these are vague words and statements that leave you with an unclear understanding.

7. After you ask a question, be quiet. Listen to what's being said. Do not think of your next question and certainly do not start talking about features and benefits.

8. Help them focus on the answer. Use the terms "define" and "explain" to focus attention on a specific subject, thereby helping the respondent elaborate rather than digress into a gripe.

CHAPTER 5

LISTENING
Letting Go of Assumptions

The first thing that you have to double down on is your customers.
You have to understand exactly what they are going through and
listen to them, probably more intently than ever before, to
understand what they're going to need in an environment like this.

—Mark Benioff

In this chapter, you'll get valuable insight into:

- ⊘ Why companies, customers, and salespeople have stopped listening
- ⊘ How the sales model has evolved in the last ten years and how that has impacted listening
- ⊘ Developing your own sales intuition and listening skills
- ⊘ How to avoid going on automatic pilot by listening with "happy ears" or pressing your own agenda

You'll learn tools and tactics to help you:

- ⊘ Use data integrity and integrate online and off-line note-taking and documentation techniques into your needs discovery strategy
- ⊘ Develop effective pain/impact questioning skills
- ⊘ Actively listen through precision questioning and paraphrasing
- ⊘ Gain the confidence of difficult telephone personalities

"They definitely need our solution, they are perfect for us. This will be a no-brainer."

"No, I didn't ask that question because I assumed when he told me he was interested in getting a quote that they were ready to buy."

"I usually write my notes on a pad of paper and forget to transfer it into my sales force automation tool. Besides, it's a hassle navigating all the fields."

"I'm not sure what he thought. He was pretty quiet during the call."

"That was a fantastic call. His entire management team was on it, interested, and asked great questions. I see bringing this deal in this month."

"The last notes I documented were back in May 2008 and I've had about ten calls since then but never logged them in. I've got it all right here in my head though, so I'm not worried."

"Oops! I forgot to log that great call a few months ago. Now I've got to call him back and try to figure it out."

LISTENING IS ABOUT TRUTH

Why has everyone stopped listening?

Customers are tired of salespeople telling them what they need, and angry at being misunderstood by quota-pressured salespeople who need to set appointments or close a deal. They are annoyed with salespeople who ask for a few minutes of their time and then abuse that time with their own agenda and never acknowledge them. Can you blame customers for rebelling by refusing to answer generic qualifying questions, or by simply refusing to take your call?

The nearly lost art of listening sits at the core of this entire book. It is the *only* skill that provides a doorway to selling from the inside out. In my trainings and in this book I take an aggressive and active approach to listening, encouraging salespeople to think intuitively and listen strategically for new opportunities.

Listening begins after we've asked some well-formulated questions. But this means *really listening*—not hearing what you want to believe, or thinking about your agenda and waiting for your turn to talk. It means actively listening to what your prospects are telling you, trying to take in what they are saying, and diving deeper into your questioning efforts.

Stop, stand still, look around, and listen up. In this chapter, I'm asking you to ask yourself the tough questions: What does your sales intuition say? Are you too busy listening for what you wish you could hear versus what is really said? Are you aware of the barriers that keep you from listening thoughtfully and trap you into reacting without thinking? What is keeping you from listening to yourself? What listening gift can you offer those close to you? What does it mean to focus on someone else's agenda versus your own for once?

LISTENING IN SALES 2.0: I CAN'T HEAR YOU NOW

By now you've got the Sales 2.0 picture: information overload, distractions, paralysis, getting noticed in a noisy market, an uncertain economy creating risk-adverse buyers. This environment does not set the stage for building a foundation of trust with solid interpersonal skills such as listening. Companies have stopped listening, customers have stopped listening, and salespeople have stopped listening. It's not surprising. When panic is pervasive and uncertainty is the norm, how can anyone take the time to listen, to believe, or to feel heard?

In the last chapter, we saw that poor listening tops the list of items that customers hate about salespeople. Customers do not feel heard from a sales and service perspective.

Salespeople continue to poorly qualify and make false sales assumptions, and in so doing they lose the possibility of really understanding their prospects.

Margaret Young's recent white paper titled "You're Not Listening to Me!" states, "In today's technology-driven market, companies are increasingly using sophisticated technologies to target and talk with high value customers and prospects. However, they may fail to implement the business practices that demonstrate that they can both listen and respond to customer needs. . . . [L]istening to customers means that we not only understand what they want, but that we can deliver what they want."

The impact of poor listening is costing organizations serious revenue dollars. As Janelle Barlow notes in her book *A Complaint Is a Gift,* when a customer is unhappy because they don't feel heard, they can spread the word within minutes through viral marketing—and bad news travels faster than good news.

Why Customers Sometimes Can't Hear You

The Sales 2.0 environment actually puts obstacles in place that prevent customers from listening.

Noise. Your customers' world is so crammed with information that they just don't have the bandwidth. Taking the time to listen to you means learning something new, and they're maxed out already. Like some salespeople, they may be conditioned to move fast and make quick decisions. Listening means they have to slow down or even stop, which just feels like wasting time. Listening also requires them to shut down the input—turn off their cell phone, stop texting on their Blackberry, and control interruptions.

Workplace Stress. Your customer may not look forward to going to work on Mondays. General workplace morale is looking pretty shaky—those who have survived layoffs and downsizing are overworked, exhausted, and panicked most of the time.

Privacy. Finally, there could be privacy issues. Customers want personalized service, but they don't want anyone to intrude on their space. Your call is just another unwelcome intrusion.

Why Salespeople Stop Listening

Customers are not the only ones. Many salespeople have also stopped listening, and for some of the same Sales 2.0 reasons.

Workplace Stress. Job stress has become a common and costly problem in the workplace. In today's economy, salespeople today are not just worried about making enough appointments and making quota, they are worried about losing the ability to ensure their family's survival.

Poor Preparation, Documentation, and Note-Taking Skills. The need for speed can cause salespeople to overlook some of the basics in their rush to make calls. Reps must learn to integrate all their information to demonstrate a stronger understanding of the prospects so they can help them feel heard and listened to. Then they must document what they've learned in their notes so they don't forget it!

Ego. A healthy ego is a necessary personality trait for a good salesperson, as is the need to conquer and be competitive. But the downside of ego is that it can lead salespeople to get defensive, reactive, and shut down their listening.

Lack of Conversational Expertise. The majority of inside salespeople are Millennials, raised with the web. They often lack expertise in building and sustaining interactive conversations, which ultimately is how a prospect feels heard.

Tools and Assumptions. The abundance of tools at our disposal can cause us to make more assumptions, quickly categorizing prospects without checking them out. We form opinions about titles, press release announcements, previously documented notes, and so on, and we come in equipped with our preconceived notions. We'll discuss the trap of listening with false assumptions in depth later in this chapter.

Metrics. If the focus is on quantity, quality suffers. When you are pressured to make a certain number of calls, the metrics keep you away from the interpersonal skills such as questioning and listening.

THE LISTENING MODEL HAS CHANGED

In the last decade, selling styles have gone through the biggest changes in their history. Markets have become more diverse. Products and services never before available are being introduced each and every day. The pace is staggering. Your customers are demanding relationships with their vendors and place a higher priority on service rendered. It's a brand new sales model.

In the past, we sold in a traditional sales model that looked something like this:

> Ten percent of selling time was establishing rapport: "Don't waste time with the customer. Get down to business."
> Twenty percent of selling time was qualification: "Find out if they have any money before you spend time on them."
> Thirty percent of the selling was presenting: "You won't be successful if you don't have 'the Gift of Gab.'"
> Forty percent of the selling time was closing technique: "Buyers are liars. Close early and often."

Today's sales approach has been transformed completely:

> Ten percent of the selling time is confirming, closing the sale, or gaining agreement to proceed. The better you handle the first part of the sale, the easier it will be to gain agreement to proceed.
> Twenty percent of the selling is presentation and demonstration of solutions that have been mutually identified as having potential to address the customer's needs.
> Thirty percent of selling time is spent in understanding and identifying needs and problems and initiating relationships.
> Forty percent of selling time is spent listening, communicating, and building rapport. Listening builds trust and credibility. The more you listen, the more the person trusts you and will open up to you. Listening increases the prospect's confidence and lowers the perception of risk.

Get Out of Your Self-Selling Utopia

Salespeople are in the doghouse. They've blown it and have been selling from what I call "self-selling utopia." It's a very comfortable, familiar, and safe place to sell from. Comfortable because you don't have to risk rejection, familiar because you mostly do all the talking, and safe because no one is going to reject you—you'll take care of that yourself! It's like telling versus selling: when the salesperson launches into "pitching" mode without taking the time to probe, listen, and present, then they are telling the prospect about a solution too soon without probing deep enough to actually sell it. When they pitch so prematurely, they risk losing their prospect because their presentation isn't aligned to the prospect's needs.

Here's how this self-selling utopia works:

The salesperson engages the prospect with an introduction, then initiates discussion by asking a strong probing question that encourages the prospect to respond. Just as the prospect begins to formulate their response, however, the salesperson interrupts by volunteering the answer, formulating another question, and attaching a quick explanation of that question. The prospect is still attempting to answer the original question before tackling the latest question, but gets sideswiped once again with a new question from the salesperson.

Surprise! The prospect stops listening and starts to look for an easy exit. But the salesperson misinterprets the silence as interest and begins to push for an appointment. By this time, the prospect is mentally exhausted and accepts an appointment simply to get the salesperson off the phone. Overjoyed, the salesperson confirms the appointment, explains what it will include, provides more information on preparing for the appointment, and asks the prospect if they have any questions. The prospect says no, in an attempt to get off the phone. The salesperson puts this appointment on the calendar and adds the prospect to a forecast that only exists in self-selling utopia.

Here's what a typical self-selling conversation sounds like:

Rep: "I'm calling to discuss your current networking needs. Can you tell me more about what you have in place?"

Prospect: "Our LAN environment is overdue for a reconfiguration. Files and data are getting lost and our end-users are not happy . . ."

Rep: "Are you familiar with the Unified Solution? Let me tell you about how it works. We are the only product in the market that works on the following platforms. Our reach is broad and some of the biggest financial verticals have the same challenges as you do. Our team of developers has put together the best suite of products and the configuration is easy to install and maintain. I assume your department is overwhelmed with requests from your end-users and we have found this to be the case, right?"

Prospect: "Well, this sounds familiar . . ."

Rep: "I'm so excited about this new product release because it is more secure than ever before. I realize that quality and reliability are critical success factors for you and that's what we deliver at our company, a name you can trust. It sounds like there are a lot of people on your network and this creates slow speed of delivery."

Prospect: "Someone has just walked into my office to remind me of a meeting, can we continue our discussion next week?"

Clearly, the rep in this dialogue lacks the questioning and listening skills required for trust and rapport to develop. Don't let this happen to you!

Listening Limitations

Selling in a nonvisual medium—over the phone or online—makes it impossible to observe body language and use eye contact. That means we have to pump up our listening skills. But most of us listen at only about 25 percent of our potential because we are distracted, preoccupied, or forgetful about 75 percent of the time. We listen at 125 to 250 words per minute but think at 1,000 to 3,000 words per minute. According to the International Listening Association, immediately after we listen to someone, we only recall about 50 percent of what the person said and, in the long term, we only remember 20 percent of what we hear.

In a face-to-face setting, we can instantly size prospects up—we notice what they are wearing, their body-type, posture, eye contact, visual signs of body art such as tattoos, and how they carry themselves. Over the phone, you can't see your listeners frowning or scowling, glancing at the clock, drumming their fingers, narrowing their eyes, folding their arms across their chest, shrugging their shoulders, rolling their eyes, hanging their heads down or shaking them, or fidgeting with their pens.

DIGGING FOR PAIN

As we mentioned in Chapter 3, "Navigating," your deal will not close if the pain or power are missing—and it's only by actively listening that you will uncover both. In today's tough economic climate, you must listen for the impact of the pain and ask yourself what the impact will be if your prospects don't implement something this month. What will they lose out on? What will happen each day they don't have something in place? That is your path to uncovering their pain and selling your solution.

Finding the pain is like having an open wound that you pour salt on: it hurts, stings, throbs . . . and that's your goal with prospects. You uncover and magnify their pain and its implications. Remember, there are two different types of pain: In dormant or latent pain, the customer doesn't realize they need something. A customer with active pain has identified and acknowledged their pain. Pain changes throughout the sales process—it grows, shrinks, and expands. Like power, it is volatile.

Salespeople usually underestimate the importance of digging for pain, or assume they are doing it. Uncovering pain is your ammunition for the call; your golden ticket if you listen consciously for an opportunity. Here is a sample roadmap with eight steps you can take to help you uncover the pain:

1. Listen to prospects' clues regarding important business challenges or issues they are having. That's where you'll find the pain.

2. Ask the prospect to describe the issue in more detail.

3. Ask the prospect to quantify these issues.

4. Ask the prospect what the consequences would be if the challenge isn't solved.

5. Check in for agreement through paraphrasing.

6. Ask how the prospect would quantify the financial impact of not solving the problem.

7. Ask the prospect to state the financial risks of not having a solution in place.

8. Lead the prospect to experience the impact of their pain.

Here's how this nine-step model works in conversation:

1. *Identify the pain:* The prospect says, "We're having a lot of problems with manual registration."

2. *Ask for more details:* "You mentioned your registration process is manual. Can you explain how you are managing this?"

3. *Ask them to quantify these issues:* "So you have fifty events per year and you usually have 150 participants per event?"

4. *Ask them what the consequences would be if the challenge isn't solved:* "How do you keep track of all the attendee data, who brought what, and who wants to attend which parts of the events?"

5. *Check for agreement through paraphrasing:* "Sounds like this can become very confusing, frustrating, and time-consuming for you!" or, "What are the disadvantages of the way you're handling this now?"

6. *Ask how they quantify the financial implication:* "How do you gauge return on investment and your time expenses on this?"

7. *What are the risks of not having a solution in place:* "What happens with this as you grow?" or, "Is this operation difficult to perform?"

8. *Have them experience the impact of their pain:* "What if you didn't have your two administrators supporting this project? What would happen?"

9. Check for agreement through paraphrasing: "Sounds like you may have to consider a solution."

Top Ten Bad Listening Habits

Listening is the toughest skill, primarily because we have never been taught to listen. Simply put, incorrect listening is all about one person waiting for their turn to talk.

Each of these listening faux pas tend to create distance and disappointment. Your listener doesn't feel heard, may get offended, and certainly shuts down.

1. Interrupting
2. Jumping to conclusions

3. Finishing the customer's sentences

4. Becoming impatient

5. Providing "me too" or "one up" interruptions

6. "All about me" listening

7. Presenting advice and solutions too soon

8. Pseudo-listening (pretending to listen)

9. Being judgmental

10. Not reacting

ACTIVE LISTENING

Active listening means really hearing what the other person is saying, evaluating it in your mind, and responding to it appropriately. It requires you to get off your agenda and get onto their agenda. Your responses can take many forms, but two types of questions dig deeper and provide you with more information: paraphrasing, and asking precision questions.

Paraphrasing

In the previous chapter, we discussed paraphrasing—restating what the person said in your own words—as a method of reflective questioning. When paraphrasing, you want to confirm and repeat back to the prospect what you just heard in your own words.

In my training, I like to play this ball-tossing game with my participants. I make a statement, throw the ball to a participant, and ask that they paraphrase what I just said. The participant listens to the statement and attempts to paraphrase, and then I ask the rest of the group if it was an accurate paraphrase. If the group responds tentatively or gingerly, I know the paraphrase was not accurate. Here is a paraphrasing example that includes both a weak and a strong paraphrase.

Statement:

> "Our decision-making process includes a committee of about eight people who come together to evaluate various solutions. I will be making the final decision and will ask that you speak with my project manager, who will be requesting an RFP."

Weak Paraphrase:

> "So you make all the decisions for eight people within your organization?"

Strong Paraphrase:

> "Let me make sure I understand you correctly. You have a team in place that evaluates and recommends vendors before requesting an RFP?"

A strong paraphrase that clearly demonstrates you are listening starts with:

"If I understand you correctly . . . ?"

"What I hear you saying is . . ."

When you want to clarify and explore the facts, ask:

"Can you clarify this?"

"Is this the problem as you see it?"

"What specifically do you mean by . . . ?"

"Do I understand correctly that you are saying . . . ?"

To check your listening accuracy, encourage further discussion by restating the prospect's basic ideas:

"As I understand it, the plan is . . . and (restatement); am I hearing you correctly?"

"I would like to make sure that . . ."

To focus the discussion and lead it to a new level, restate, reflect, and summarize major ideas and feelings:

"If I heard you correctly, these are the key elements of the problem: . . ."

"Let's see now, we've covered . . ."

"If I understand, you feel this way about the situation . . ."

To indicate that you empathize with the prospect's feelings, make statements such as:

"I can appreciate that . . ."

"It sounds like you are under a tight timeline. Let me help."

"I can understand how frustrated you must feel."

"I'm sorry that happened."

A simple question that invites the prospect to "tell me more about that" can be asked in ten ways:

1. "Why is that?"
2. "What are your ideas (opinions, thoughts) on _____?"
3. "What did you mean when you said _____?"
4. "Why is that important (essential, relevant)?"
5. "How does that look (feel, seem) to you?"
6. "What are some examples of _____?"
7. "What's your definition of _____?"
8. "Can you elaborate on _____?"
9. "What does _____ mean for you?"
10. "Can you share with me how you_____?"

Asking Precision Questions

In order to reveal your prospects' true needs and help you understand the issues they raise, you'll want to ask about specifics by using precision questions. Precision questions usually start with:

"How specifically do you . . . ?"

"What exactly is your goal . . . ?"

In probing and needs discovery, salespeople often encounter a lot of fuzzy words that obscure the customer's real needs and objectives. By listening and asking precision questions about these fuzzy words, you can turn a "brush-off" into a meaningful discovery. We will discuss more precision questions in Chapter 8, "Handling Objections."

The following five statements include fuzzy words. To test your understanding of asking precision questions, circle the fuzzy words and then formulate a precision question. Answers are supplied below.

1. "We have the budget to get this, but I haven't had the time to review your quote with my staff."

2. "We're excited about this technology and think that six months down the road, we'll implement something."

3. "We can get this solution free as a bundled solution."

4. "We are completely standardized on this."

5. "You guys are way too expensive! I need a discount. I need to cost justify this and show a price reduction to my boss before doing anything."

Answers:

1. **We have** the **budget** to **get this**, but I **haven't had the time** to **review** your quote with **my staff**. (Examples of precision questions: "Please define who 'we' is?" "What type of budget has been determined for this project?" "What is your review process?" "Please help me understand what individuals on your staff are part of this process.")

2. We're **excited** about **this technology** and **think** that **six months down the road, we'll implement something**. (Examples of precision questions: "Great to hear that you are excited; what exactly do you find exciting about our technology?" "What do you mean by six months down the road?" "What exactly will you be implementing?")

3. We **can get this** solution **free as a bundled solution**. (Examples of precision questions: "Please tell me what components are bundled in

this solution?" "Let me better understand 'free'—what are you comparing this to?" "For what timeframe will this be free?")

4. We are **completely standardized** on **this**. (Examples of precision questions: "Let me better understand what you mean by standardized? Across product lines? Platforms? Departments?" "Who made the decision to standardize?")

5. **You guys** are **way too expensive**! I **need** a **discount**. I **need** to **cost-justify** this and **show a price reduction** to **my boss** before **doing anything**. (Examples of precision questions: "What are you finding to be too expensive?" "What are you comparing us to?" "How will you proceed in your cost justification?" "What type of cost reduction are you looking for?")

USING VERBAL LISTENING CUES

As we mentioned earlier, visuals are nonexistent when you are on the phone, but everyone uses listening cues to acknowledge the conversation. There is, however, a danger in sticking with the same listening cues over and over, such as "uh huh, uh huh, uh huh, uh huh, uh huh," or "okay, okay, okay, okay, okay," or even this one that I recently heard: "wow, wow, wow, wow." You must vary these listening cues to demonstrate strong active listening techniques. Words such as "excellent," "good," "yes," "right," "sure," and "definitely" are all encouraging and motivating and signal that you have been paying attention to what they are saying.

LISTENING WITHOUT ASSUMPTIONS

In sales, after making hundreds of calls to prospects who have similar needs, we assume we know what they need and stop listening. We have a great conversation with a prospect who really likes our product or service and explains how perfect it is for them right now, and we assume they will buy. But when we listen with assumptions, we clearly are not listening. We also call this listening with "happy ears," a sales term to describe hearing what we want to believe. Depending on the time of the month, the salesperson, or the customer, it's easy for sales-people to listen with "happy ears."

Assumptions are something we think or believe or assume will happen. We play out a scenario in our mind that isn't verified or proven and then we get tangled up because we add expectations and set ourselves up for disappointment. All this because we assumed something that wasn't true. Remember that assumptions are not fact based; they are what we *want* to believe, so we are quick to jump to a conclusion without checking it out. Assumptions can get us into real trouble because they make us stop listening. Spend more time in the moment and less time on how you want the situation to be.

SALES INTUITION

How often do you listen to your intuition? Some people are naturally more intuitive than others, and some just need to develop this sense. But we all have it. It's that tiny voice that nudges you when something is wrong, pushes you when something is really wrong, and hits you over the head when you have completely messed up.

How many times have we heard people say, *"I knew it from the minute I met him or spoke with him,"* or *"Right from the start, I knew something wasn't right"*? These are critical intuitive signals. Pay atten-tion!

BECOMING COMFORTABLE WITH THE SILENT PAUSE

When you are on the phone, pausing means you are waiting in silence, listening, and not jumping in at the first opportunity. When we have such little time on the phone, it is typical for inside salespeople to lose confidence in this technique, mostly because they are not sure when to pause, or for how long. The best listening happens when you are authentically curious about what your prospect is saying. This will cause you to pause automatically. You ask a question, pause, wait for the answer, and really listen to it. When the speaker stops for a moment, pause again instead of rushing in. You'll both win, because the speaker gets a chance to finish his or her thoughts and feel validated, and you're more likely to get valuable information that you might not receive otherwise. The longest recorded pause in inside sales history lasted about forty seconds—and that was after a closing question!

Here are some benefits to pausing:

> Your customers can stop to gather their thoughts or to take a breath.

> Your prospects may be gauging your interest in their point of view, or checking to see if you're listening, or simply waiting to jump in. When you resist the urge to jump in, you are often pleasantly surprised to hear that there's more, and that it is important.

> Most people feel uncomfortable with silence, so they rush in to fill the void. Instead of rushing in, by pausing you can give your customers a chance to fill the void.

> Your customers feel validated and important when you give them a chance to elaborate on their thoughts.

> Silence carries the control and power on the call, if used methodically.

NOTE TAKING IS INFORMATION CAPTURE

Another part of listening is remembering what you heard. That means documenting information from your discussion. This is an investment of time and energy that builds trust and relationships. Having the correct information earns you time on your call. The more information you can bring, the more time you will earn.

Inside sales warriors are becoming data hounds. They must be comfortable gathering data, synthesizing it, and integrating it into their next call. One of the greatest advantages of being on the phone is that you can take detailed notes unobserved. Taking notes can be the telephone equivalent of in-person eye contact. Not only will taking notes help you focus, it will help you position yourself by organizing your client's words and ideas on paper.

Here are some tips for good note taking:

> Handwrite your notes. Your brain will focus more than if you are typing on a keyboard while talking with your prospect.

> Draw a listening map to get visual and expand your way of listening. This is similar to Tony Buzan's work on mind mapping. The map starts with a core idea in the center, and you attach a new box or circle to the periphery each time you add a new thought or idea. This creativity technique is used to capture notes and expand your listening capabilities by remembering what to ask.

> Draw circles, stars, or boxes around key words or points mentioned during the call and use them as a reminder of something you want to ask.

> After the call, transfer the information into your database immediately. Don't let your notes pile up for the end of the day.

> Learn to succinctly enter the notes in the database. Too much information can be just as damaging as too little information. This is critical and sets you up for your next call.

YOU ARE ONLY AS GOOD AS YOUR NOTES

If you were to inherit someone's territory and needed to get up to speed on the account, which notes would be most useful? A or B?

A: 6/30/06—Spoke with JB, who was rushed. Said they are still interested and to try back in a few weeks. Liked the demo, too.

B: 6/30/06—JB is the Director of IT. He reports to Bob Smith, who is the VP of IT. Their team has about sixteen people and JB is taking the lead on this project. He attended the demo session and thought our new upgrades were perfect for their needs and wants to get Bob involved on this. Bob isn't as familiar with our solution and is a big Oracle guy but open to new technologies. JB has a lot of influence with Bob. They want to move on something within the next ninety days because that's the end of their fiscal. They will include the CFO on this because he will be funding this.

If you said B, you're right. There is enough information in this scenario for you to come in with a sense of familiarity and open the dialogue by integrating this information into your opening statement. It also helps you prepare your questions to JB, Bob Smith, and the CFO.

Good notes earn time. Here are some tips for pumping up your documentation:

- Sync up with your manager to determine what fields to fill out.
- Sync up with your field partners to make sure they review the notes you input.
- Document your notes immediately after getting off the call; don't delay or get up to get a cup of coffee.
- Take notes based on the eight qualification criteria noted in Chapter 4, "Questioning."
- Include enough information to help you formulate your opening statement on your next call.
- Learn to quickly access your notes before and during a call.
- Don't create spreadsheets to complement your notes. You will soon get scattered managing disparate systems. Stick to one central repository when it comes to documenting information.

INFORMATION INTEGRATION

Information integration is about integrating data, contact, or notes into your conversation. It is a technique that doesn't get that much attention, yet it has been proven to score major points in discussion with prospects. Information earns you time on the phone, which means your prospect is willing to listen and has agreed to be qualified. Here are some tips for integrating information:

- Proper note taking is valuable in helping you set up for your next call. The more information you *bring* equals the more time you will *earn* on the call.
- You must *give* information in order to *receive*.

> In the beginning of the call, try to *balance* the information you have, establishing rapport and gaining cooperation. Remember that too much information may confuse or lose your prospect.

> *Easy* and *quick* access to information is key to strong information integration. Good note taking and a good memory help a lot too.

Cubicle Chronicles

——————— Dealing with Difficult Telepersonalities: Listening Tips———————

We never know who will answer that phone. Within seconds, however, we must quickly align and acknowledge. Difficult prospects present a real challenge in this regard. When you have an angry customer, you want to align with them—not mirror their personality. If you want to earn points with these difficult folks, here are some dos and don'ts:

DO	DON'T
Allow ample time for response	Automatically give advice
Use short responses	Pretend to understand
Tailor response to caller	Respond with a cliché
Use an even tone of voice	Sound condescending
Consider their point of view	Jump to conclusions
Mirror their tone and attitude	Mimic their speech and mannerisms

Here are some specific response techniques you can use with difficult telephone personalities:

Fast Freddy is quick and expects answers now. Everything is urgent for him and he becomes impatient quickly.

Listening Tip: Use an equal amount of urgency in your voice, but propose action. Help him differentiate between what is urgent and what is important. Stay focused, clear, and organized.

Sarcastic Sue has a sharp bite and can be condescending and abrasive.

Listening Tip: Stay composed and do not get intimidated or angry. Be reassuring and give a confident and knowledgeable response.

Pleasant Paul is outgoing, friendly, and naturally blessed with a good disposition. But he likes to chat and tends to move off track.

Listening Tip: Mirror his outgoing and friendly style. Exchange some small talk, but get him back on track quickly.

Skeptical Sally's motto is "This will never work." Her nay-saying attitude is not a sign that she mistrusts you. It shows her fear of change and need to be seen as an expert.

Listening Tip: Don't become defensive. Think of her objections as an opportunity to sell your solution. Thank her for bringing up insightful issues and reassure her that your solution will minimally disrupt her status quo.

Angry Alan is upset by the slightest problem. He jumps to negative conclusions quickly and feeds off conflict situations.

Listening Tip: Do not get defensive. Respond positively, stay calm, and give him time to vent. Listen to him and acknowledge his efforts. Position yourself as an ally with your solutions.

Detailed Diane speaks precisely and may overwhelm you with the sheer amount of information she relays.

Listening Tip: Mirror her detailed nature by actively listening and tracking all the facts. Take control of the call by clearly stating which details will take priority.

Clueless Cameron is easily confused and is disorganized in his approach.

Listening Tip: Be patient and caring. Clarify, clarify, clarify. Always rephrase his questions, help him focus, and meet him at his knowledge level and help educate him.

Know-It-All Norma believes that she has "been there and done that." She may just be pretending that she knows it all, but she might actually know a great deal. Either way, she is looking for validation of her intelligence and experience.

Listening Tip: Acknowledge her wisdom, then use precision questions to try to distinguish what she does and does not know. Accept her help on what she does know, and always thank her for her expertise.

LISTENING STRATEGIES

1. Adopt strong listening techniques and appropriate verbal responses that encourage needs discovery and establish trust.

2. To better understand prospects, think like them and listen to their point of view.

3. Don't be judgmental and dismiss prospects' ideas if you don't agree with them.

4. Don't interrupt, and particularly avoid "me too" interruptions.

5. Remember not to "tell," but "sell"—limit your own talking. Speak 30 percent of the time and listen 70 percent of the time.

6. Practice active listening techniques such as paraphrasing and asking precision questions.

7. Take good notes. Draw a listening map to fully understand the message.

8. Make information capture your biggest priority. Keep your notes field in your database up to date and include details.

9. Make sure you are not listening with "happy ears."

10. Become comfortable with silence.

CHAPTER 6

LINKING
Selling to Power Buyers

Take risks. Ask big questions. Don't be afraid to make mistakes; if you don't make mistakes, you're not reaching far enough.

—David Packard

In this chapter, you'll get valuable insight into:
- What fears keep you from calling at the highest level within an organization
- The importance of influence as a major factor in the decision-making process
- How Sales 2.0 has redefined power
- Why we sabotage ourselves from connecting with power buyers

You'll learn tools and tactics to help you:
- Align with influence
- Recognize power buyers over the phone and on e-mail
- Get comfortable with the altitude at C-level
- Turn to the "alpha" influencer, the executive assistant
- Spot power through the org chart and understand the hidden meaning of power
- Adjust your language and message to different titles within the corporate hierarchy
- Practice daily affirmations to boost your confidence and self-esteem

I hear comments like these whenever I coach salespeople who are accustomed to speaking with No-Po's and don't have the guts to talk with the power buyers:

"I didn't know what to say! He just happened to answer the phone and I froze. I was prepared to speak with his executive assistant. Catching a CEO on the phone was a surprise."

"There's no way I'll get through that army of gatekeepers who screen her."

"I finally learned more about the committee that makes decisions on these purchases and made an appointment with them for the middle of next month."

"I usually tag-team with my field partner, who discourages me from calling high because that's where he wants to hang out. Instead, he wants me to get it ready at the lower level."

"Awesome! I found out she pulls the trigger on all IT purchases worldwide. Now I just have to get to her and see if she'll give me the time of day."

"The demo was moving along well until the boss jumped on the call. It completely changed the dynamics. That caught me off-guard."

"No, the CEO doesn't even know about my company, nor does he care."

LINKING CONNECTS YOU WITH C-LEVEL DECISION MAKERS

Sales reps are often uncomfortable with calling high—talking to the *real* decision makers, not the No-Po's. It's ironic, but it's also no surprise: these busy execs can be unforgiving if they're approached in the wrong way. Reps who fail to capture their attention—or somehow offend them—are shown the virtual door pretty quickly.

Let's take a brief look at your sales journey so far. In Chapter 1, "Time Management," you learned skills to help you prioritize your time with decision makers. In Chapter 2, "Introducing," you learned the key messaging essentials you need to hold your weight on an introductory call. In Chapter 3, "Navigating," you learned how easily you can be led astray if you inadvertently use these great skills with a No-Po instead of a power player. In Chapter 4, "Questioning," you learned ways to quickly identify the power potential of the person you are talking with. And, in Chapter 5, "Listening," you learned to listen for their pain. But none of these great skills will get you anywhere if you haven't figured out how to connect with the power players who reside at C-level: CEOs, CFOs, CTOs, CMOs, COOs. Your forecast will always suffer if you haven't properly messaged your value proposition and strategically aligned enough power buyers. In this chapter, you'll learn the skill that brings the others together and raises your game to the next level: linking.

Why Sales Reps *Don't* Call High

There are many reasons why salespeople engage in self-sabotage—not connecting well, or not even making the call—instead of linking strongly with the power buyer. Here are just a few:

> *They are deluded.* They believe they are doing fine without the power player.

> *They are lost.* They don't know where to find the power players, or don't recognize them if they do find them (by accident, usually).

> *They fear No-Po backlash.* They want to be loyal to their No-Po, who has requested that they don't call his or her boss.

> *They are insecure.* They feel uncomfortable, know they will get pushed back down, and don't have a strong enough value proposition to keep them holding their ground.

> *They feel powerless.* They would prefer that their manager call the power source, because they've been taught that power breeds power, and they feel it's better to have the heavy hitters go at it together.

> *They believe the "Do not disturb" sign on the door.* They are convinced that the person at the top is completely unavailable, and they're too inconsequential to get in.

> *They think there are too many skillful bodyguards.* They can't get past the power player's many gatekeepers.

> *Words fail them.* They don't know what to say, what to talk about, and cannot hold their weight with the appropriate language and conversational skills.

> *They feel more confident and in their comfort zone talking to No-Pos.* This is a real tip-off that they are insecure and lack the personal power to connect with power players.

Later in this chapter, we'll learn some ways to get around the most insidious gatekeeper: yourself!

Learn the Linking Skills That Make Calling High Successful

This chapter is not just about calling high and getting to the C-level decision maker. It's about knowing how to respond when they say "Hello?" You'll learn how to speak their special language and enter into a "members-only" club where you are no longer seen as a vendor but as a *solutions provider*, a valued consultant they rely on when defining their short- and long-term business strategies. But more importantly, effective linking is about *believing* you deserve to be talking with the power players, and learning how to move the mountains that get in your way.

SALES 2.0 HAS REDEFINED POWER

As we established in our discussion of navigating in Chapter 3, you can't always assume you know who has the power just by reading an org chart. In Sales 2.0, power is an invisible force that moves and hides. And increasingly, more players than ever are stepping into the decision-making process. According to Miller Heiman's Executive Summary of their "2008 Sales Best Practices Study," you must be prepared to convince a committee of up to six or more decision makers during your sales process. The highest level won't just rubberstamp your deal: they may get involved in the buying process, too.

In the past, these committees were department specific. In a typical committee, you might find the director of IT, the manager of IT, and an IT administrator making decisions. Today's committee is different. It may include people from IT, marketing, sales, finance, support, training, and operations. And these committees want proof that your solution works. According to Landslide's 2008 white paper "Give Me Something I Can Use":

> Salespeople have to navigate ever more complex purchasing behaviors, thanks to process safeguards like committee-based reviews and

approvals, mandated demonstration of return on investment, required proof-of-concept trials and more. One thing that hasn't changed is salespeople have to understand and address the buying needs and objectives of the economic buyers, business buyers, technical buyers and end-users.

Sales 2.0 has redefined power. People no longer swarm around a single omnipotent power buyer, praying for that person to sign off. Instead, power resides in a diverse committee of power players representing different departments, from technical to financial to nuts and bolts, each with its own focus. But make no mistake: these people are still high level, and calling them means calling high.

Authority versus Influence

Not all these power players hide behind big titles and years of experience. They are the new corporate renegades, the thought leaders, the mavericks who can traverse the playing field—talking technology one minute and business strategy the next. They're not afraid to influence change, and they're being rewarded for it. They may not have the budget dollars in hand, but they know how to get them.

To understand who has power, the first step is to separate those with authority from those with influence. *Authority* is power that is granted, and *influence* is power that is earned. People with high authority can have big titles—like CEO, CFO, or CMO. These people also control the budget dollars. But, as you probably know, getting to these people usually isn't a matter of cold-calling them. Instead, you need to align with someone who has high influence—such as their VP, director, or managers—who can help you manage the power and get to the person with high authority.

Align Yourself with Influence

Aligning yourself with the person who has the power to influence someone with authority to spend the dollars should be your top priority. Knowing who has influence means using your navigating skills to identify the people who drive sales. By now it should be crystal clear why we want to avoid No-Po's at all costs: not only do they not have authority, *they lack influence.* Influencers may not have authority, but they don't need it to influence the decision-making process!

You may see this dynamic at work in your own family. At your next family reunion, when all the aunts and uncles, cousins, and grandparents are together, stand back and observe the interaction. Watch for the sources of power in the gathering. Who is in a high authority role? It's usually the eldest—the grandfather, the matriarch, or even the oldest brother or sister—who everyone looks to for approval and authority. Now look for those who have influence. These people are usually easy to spot: the clever cousin who everyone goes to for advice, or the very popular aunt who orchestrates celebrations (such as the one you are attending!), or the favorite uncle who is the most popular guy in the room and the real reason you decided to attend this event. You can use this familiar model as you navigate through an organization, looking for people with authority and influence to link with.

How to Know if You're in the High-Influence Zone

Power is invisible, but high-influence power buyers can be identified. Look for the following qualities when searching for power buyers:

- ➤ Personal prestige: success record
- ➤ Personal credibility: how much trust they generate
- ➤ Technical credibility: ability to comprehend and fix the problem
- ➤ Personal vision: a clear idea of what winning looks like
- ➤ Weight: the amount they have to "throw around," if necessary
- ➤ Alliances: who they are able to influence that controls resources
- ➤ Consultative capacity: how they engage with others to convince
- ➤ Communication skill: talent for rational persuasion
- ➤ Inspirational appeal: ability to "sell" vision to others

HOW TO SPOT THE POWER BUYERS

Power buyers are powerful decision makers with both purchasing influence *and* buying authority. They have a high-level understanding of the technical as well as the business needs in their department and organization, and they can influence the decision up, down, and out. Why? Because they have a vision.

Power buyers have exceptional communication skills. They are extremely articulate over e-mail and on the phone. They can easily and quickly access the highest level for a meeting or review, and ultimately have influence in speeding up the decision-making process. And they are more likely to buy based on what *you* know about their company and business rather than on what *they* know about your solution.

Usually, they are stretched in many directions—invited to participate in numerous meetings, and involved in multiple committees. They are well liked and highly respected, they are effective at time management, delegating, and using their resources to best effect. They have earned a very high level of influence and credibility and want to be approached with the highest level of respect and knowledge. They are decisive, have the power to make things happen, and know how to find the budget dollars.

Using the Org Chart to Find Hidden Power

Have you ever played "Where's Waldo"? It can be hard to find the little guy amid all the distractions in the drawings. But when you realize you have to look for Waldo's red-and-white-striped shirt, your task becomes a lot easier. Finding the power buyer hidden in the org chart has a lot in common with this game. And as with Waldo's shirt, knowing what to look for will help you navigate the chart quickly.

Within every organization there is an invisible power structure that has little to do with org charts. When we look at an org chart we can either look at it as the names and hierarchical titles or as the political undercurrents of influence.

Figure 6-1 is a typical organizational chart for the ABC Company. This chart includes many titles—some high level, some low level—and

Figure 6-1. Org Chart Analysis

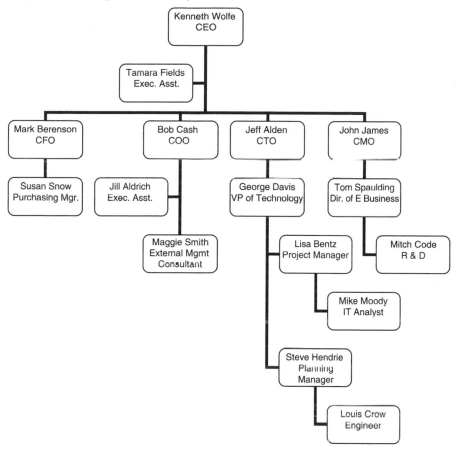

individuals who lack power, and others who lack influence. (Remember that just because someone has a high-level title doesn't necessarily mean they have influence.)

As an exercise, review the following clues about each person in the org chart in Figure 6-1. Try to determine whether they have influence (mark the box in the chart with "I") or authority (mark the box with "A"), or whether they are a No-Po (mark the box with "NP"). This is exactly what you would do if you were navigating a real org chart.

Kenneth Wolfe: The board brought him in to salvage the company.
Tamara Fields: She has been Kenneth's executive assistant for the past fifteen years.

Mark Berenson: He is very old school, conservative, and ready to retire.

Bob Cash: He came from the competition and has been brought in to start a global initiative.

Jeff Alden: His organization messed up a huge e-commerce deployment—the project was delayed eight months and cost the company $1.5 million over budget.

John James: His department's budget has been reduced by 20 percent.

Susan Snow: Her promotions are based on her ability to discount and negotiate with vendors.

Jill Aldrich: She supports several key executive managers.

George Davis: He is the implementer of the company's e-commerce technology.

Tom Spaulding: He is Kenneth's Wolfe's brother-in-law, is very quick, and is on a fast career track.

Maggie Smith: She is currently assessing the entire department.

Lisa Bentz: She manages key projects for George Davis.

Mitch Code: He understands R&D and is very visionary.

Mike Moody: He is knee-deep in managing the technical aspects of the e-commerce technology.

Louis Crow: He has ideas to improve e-commerce technology, but no one is paying attention.

Steve Hendrie: He is Tamara Fields's nephew.

How well did you do? Read the following to see if you spotted the I's, A's, and NP's correctly, and review the explanations.

Kenneth Wolfe: I and A
His high ranking as CEO of the company gives him authority. The board selected him to salvage the company, so he also has high influence.

Tamara Fields: I
Her tenure of fifteen years and the fact that she reports to the CEO gives her high influence. She is also a potent source of information.

Mark Berenson: A
The CFO title gives him automatic authority; but the fact that

he is ready to retire and is "old school and conservative" doesn't give him much influence.

Bob Cash: I and A

He walks in with high influence since he came from the competition, and he's automatically in a high authority role because of his title.

Jeff Alden: extremely limited A

Although he was in a position of high authority, his recent e-commerce fiasco has placed him in a negative power position.

John James: limited A

He has authority but lacks influence, since his budget was cut.

Susan Snow: A

Purchasing managers only work with the budget they have at hand—they rarely have influence over the budget.

Jill Aldrich: I

If someone supports multiple executives that's a good sign of influence, since they are in demand for their great communication skills.

George Davis: NP

Although he has an impressive title (VP of Technology), we cannot be fooled into believing he has influence or authority. He doesn't have any direct reports and has been asked to implement a solution that leaves little room for influence.

Tom Spaulding: I

He has high influence because of his family connection with the president of the company; and because he is on a career track, he is receiving support. He may not have a budget but, as a director, he knows where to go to find it.

Maggie Smith: I

External consultants often have a lot of influence because they've been hired to fix problems.

Lisa Bentz: NP

Project managers make sure everything runs on track, but they don't spend money.

Mitch Code: I

He understands R&D from a higher level and his vision puts him into a high-influence role.

Mike Moody: NP

He doesn't have authority or influence, but since he is knee-deep in managing projects, he is a No-Po. Your solution may threaten the viability and longevity of his job, so he may be invested in keeping you away.

Louis Crow: NP

The fact that Louis cannot find anyone to pay attention to him makes him a No-Po.

Steve Hendrie: I

He has influence because of his family connection with Tamara, who is the president's executive assistant.

Recognizing Power Buyers over the Phone

In Chapter 3, "Navigating," you learned that figuring out who might be the power buyer is a lot easier in person than it is over the phone in your cubicle. It would be great if prospects told you the amount of power they really hold in an organization when they answer their phone—and they actually can, if you just ask them. Your navigating and questioning skills come into play here to help you ask the right questions to determine the level of influence of the person you're speaking with. Each question in the following list includes an example of an answer that tells you whether they have influence or authority:

- How long have you been with your organization? *"I've been here nine years."*
- How long have you been in your current role? *"I've held several different positions over the years that have crossed into multiple departments."*
- What types of projects do you usually get involved with? *"I'm usually brought in to fix messes, assemble teams, ramp them up, and then go elsewhere."*
- Do you get involved on other initiatives within the organizations? *"Too many! I've got to cut down on my involvement."*
- Who usually drives these types of projects? *"It depends. I'm usually the one to get it started and come in at the end once it's complete."*

> What is your role in the decision-making process? *"I influence and recommend."*
> Can you walk me through your decision-making process, from the research stage to the implementation stage? *"I come in at the idea and recommendation stage and delegate the research and implementation parts."*
> Why have you been delegated this task? *"My tenure with this company and my knowledge of various departments puts me in a high-visibility role."*

LINKING WITH INFLUENTIAL EXECUTIVE ASSISTANTS

Rather than trying to bulldoze your way past an army of gatekeepers, it's more effective—and far less frustrating—to create allies. Often, that means courting the influential executive assistant.

According to a 2008 Monster.com salary survey, high-level administrative assistants working for a Fortune 500 company assisting a C-level executive are making well over $100,000 per year. Why? Because they are not just glorified secretaries screening their boss's calls. They are "alpha" influencers, doing everything from arranging corporate retreats to sitting in on board meetings to organizing an executive briefing. They are also invaluable and irreplaceable, which explains why they will follow their executive around throughout his or her career. So, when you get an executive assistant on the phone, the first question you want to ask them is, "How long have you been working with (the C-level decision maker)?" The more years, the greater their influence, and the more effective an ally for you to link with.

Talking Points

Now you can begin to establish a relationship with the assistant. As you do, keep in mind the following points:

> Remember that their job is to protect the decision maker's time, so don't be put off if they don't let you in right away.
> Treat them like allies, not secretaries: show respect, learn their names.
> Ask for help: "I'm wondering if you can help me." Remember that you are not selling your product at that moment.

> Assist them by giving them exactly what they want, when they want it, in the exact order in which they want it.

> Humanize the interaction by being direct, honest, and straightforward. Be very clear about exactly what you want.

> Be aware of your voice tone and be confident. Give verbal hugs, but don't be too squishy!

> Listen for subtle clues about your decision maker—you'll use them to link effectively when you finally get the boss on the phone.

> Be fast and quick when asking questions—no one in the company has less time to waste than the executive assistant!

> Talk about "needs" instead of "wants," and be specific about what you need.

Invited In or Shut Out?

The way you approach the executive assistant can quickly get them to open the door—perhaps even e-mailing you an org chart on the spot!—or shut you out completely. Review the following ten conversation starters and determine which will keep you out or let you in:

1. "I need to speak with Ron Pollis. Can you please put me through?"

2. "I wonder if you can help me . . ."

3. "Hi . . . sounds like you're having a hectic day. Listen, well . . . um . . . umm, I'm wondering if you can answer a few questions."

4. "Do you have a minute to answer a few questions?"

5. "My name is _____ and I'm preparing some information for _____."

6. "I just spoke with _____'s office, who directed me to you."

7. "Hi, what's your name? I am with ABC Company and we are the leaders in . . . I need your help today with . . ."

8. "Can you transfer me to someone in the IT department?"

9. "I have about six names here. Can you help me update these?"

10. "I have tried calling Bob and have left numerous messages with you. Why can't you help me out?"

How did you do? Review the following answers and explanations:

1. Shut out. You are not offering them anything, so why should they help you?

2. Invited in. This magic phrase—"I wonder if you can help me . . ."—virtually guarantees access because it is neither defensive nor offensive.

3. Shut out. You've already used up your time to connect. You must keep the conversation moving forward when talking with an EA.

4. Shut out. This is a closed-ended question, and they have no idea what you will be asking them. They will always use their easy out: "No."

5. Invited in. When you identify yourself and explain what you need, it disarms them and puts them in a position to help.

6. Invited in. If you name-drop someone within the organization, it locates you in a chain of influence and heightens your credibility.

7. Shut out. EAs don't respond well to "salesy" or phony tactics.

8. Shut out. They have no idea who you need and why you are calling and frankly they don't care.

9. Shut out. Six names is a lot to ask of a busy person you don't have a relationship with yet. Perhaps start with two or three. If the conversation goes well, you can ask for a few more.

10. Shut out. This kind of whiny complaint is unnecessary and annoying. They will probably hang up on you.

SPOTTING POWER BUYERS THROUGHOUT THE SALES CYCLE

You've already learned how to spot a No-Po: Things seem to drag along, you get vague responses, they waste your time with useless requests, and they're never able to make a real decision. Power buyers can also be easy to spot by the way they respond on the phone or via e-mail.

Power buyers frequently identify themselves in what (and how) they write in e-mail. And that's fortunate, because in a Sales 2.0 environment, the majority of your powerful contacts will communicate using their BlackBerry or other PDAs. Let's walk you through the entire sales process from beginning to the end so you can see these characteristics in action.

Early in the Sales Cycle: They're Quick and Take Action

Power buyers got to the top by being quick on the uptake, and they don't have time to waste. You can recognize them from the following behaviors:

> *They get right to the point.* Power buyers usually aren't big schmoozers. They ask only a couple of key questions, from a broad perspective. They want to know how your product or service will impact their organization at a high level. They'll ask you to link technical or operational issues to strategic and political benefits—or will do so themselves, because they're quick on their feet and always thinking about the bottom line.

> *They make it simple.* Power buyers know how to present. They can make complex problems simple. They know how to build a business case, and they easily persuade the people around them to share their view. When you witness a power buyer explaining your solution, you'll want to take notes—because chances are, they'll do it better than you do. They're informed about other funded projects and initiatives, and their decisions are quick, confident, and knowledgeable. (If you run into a No-Po that does this, don't write them off forever—they'll probably be in a position of influence sooner rather than later!)

> *They take action.* Make sure they understand your request. Unlike No-Po's (who ask lots of questions and make lots of requests, or simply try to keep you out without trying to learn anything about you at all), power buyers will take action immediately by asking you to schedule time on their calendar with their assistant, or they'll refer you to one of their direct reports. For example:

```
Judy,
Can you give Lee thirty mins on my calendar the week
of the 27th?

Thanks,
Fred
```

Phil,

Thanks for reaching out. I've cc'd Keller on your
e-mail since he oversees this function globally.

Thank you.
Joan

Mid-Sales Cycle: They Refer You to Their Team

Most large purchases are now made by committee. But the power
buyer has final purchasing authority among a group or committee of
decision makers. They may oversee the committee tasked to research
the solution; they may also be part of the committee that oversees the
purchase.

Because the powerful aren't worried about protecting their turf,
and because they're overly busy, they'll refer you to work with people
on their team. Whom they delegate to and whom they refer you to is
key: it reflects how much importance they place on your services. *If
they refer you to the powerless, they are brushing you off. But if they refer you
to their direct report or executive assistant, they are interested and want to
pursue a meeting with you.*

Don't expect to hear from your power buyer during the middle of
the sales cycle. Power buyers don't require much hand-holding—
they're fairly decisive and candid about their process. If you ask for a
status update, you may not hear back from them immediately. But
when you do, it may be detailed and actionable. Here's a sample
response from a status update:

Hi,

Please continue to work with Laura Rodney on this.

Thanks

End of the Sales Cycle: They Keep Their Commitments

It's not easy to get a powerful buyer to commit. But if they do, it's
solid. They'll give you action steps, they'll stick to their promise, and
they'll do what it takes to execute and make it happen fast.

Hi,

I got your message and I'm on the road until next
week. I'm looking at bringing you in for a two-day
training in Atlanta the week of March 8th. Please
provide me with your avail.

Thanks
Norm

ACCESS GRANTED! NOW WHAT?

It's one thing to know who the power buyer is, but contacting them
directly is a different matter entirely. As we saw in Chapter 2, "Introducing," when top decision makers were asked what they considered
to be strong introductions, most of them said the same thing: the
sales rep did his or her homework. One CEO told me, "I'll let them
in once, but if they don't offer value in the call, I will probably delegate them to others or simply nor respond." If you gain access—and
want to continue the relationship—the following are keys to your success.

Live and Breathe Their World

This is where your precall research comes to life—not just from gathering a bunch of names, but from learning what type of company it
is and how it is positioned in the marketplace. Research recent press
releases, company mission statements, and shareholder meeting
minutes, and watch videos of their new announcements. Blogs are a
perfect way to get insight on their corporate strategy and position—
especially if written by the CEO. Review everything, and synthesize
the information with your solution. Become part of the conversation,
because only when you've done your homework are you ready to
make some calls.

Only when you've done your homework are you ready to make
some calls.

The Org Chart: Your Power Playlist

You may be able to make some very good guesses by looking at the org chart, but the only way you're going to confirm your hunches is with hard information. As you learned in the chapter on navigating, you may discover that some of the really hopeful prospects you saw on the company's chart have gone on to new positions, or that others have power in name only. When you're ready to pick up the phone and link with power, this information becomes critical.

For example, here's how you might work the ABC Company org chart we used earlier in this chapter with a series of strategic calls aimed at getting marketing dollars:

> ➤ Start by calling the CEO's executive assistant to confirm that John James is the CMO. Find out how big his team is and confirm who his players are.
>
> ➤ You already know that Lisa Bentz is probably a No-Po, but she can be an easy source of information at this point. Make an initial intro call just to figure out the landscape, uncover potential needs, and confirm team members. Remember to move away from her after you are equipped with information you need.
>
> ➤ George Davis is likely another No-Po, but you can learn his relation to Jeff Alden, what his goals are, and how much he knows about your solution. In talking to George, incorporate whatever information you have learned from Lisa Bentz. Don't stick around too long with George either.

See how one call builds on the other to give you complex layers of information? The more information you have, the more quickly you can zero in on your best prospect. Sometimes, just one phone call can give you all the information you need to identify your No-Po's, gather nuggets of gold, and find the route to your power buyer. This actual navigation call demonstrates the linking skill in action:

Smart Seller: "Hi, Beth. I'm Larry Brown, with Acme Corp. I'm hoping you can point me in the right direction. I've been in touch with Lisa Track and Ingrid Breem in the past. Does John Jones still report to them?"

Beth: "Lisa and Ingrid are your best bet—John's no longer with the company."

Smart Seller: "Okay, interesting. What about Julie Fox and Tom Demata?"

Beth: "Actually, Julie's on maternity leave and Tom is my counterpart. We both report to Ingrid."

Smart Seller: "Thanks, you've been so helpful. The puzzle is starting to make more sense. So your role is . . . ?"

Beth: "I'm in charge of the enablement group, but we don't have access to any budget. Everything rolls up to Ingrid for final approval. We support Ingrid's initiatives and manage the vendors."

Smart Seller: "You are so knowledgeable and helpful—I really appreciate it. What's the best way for me to reach Ingrid?"

Beth: "She's out the next few days, but I know she'll be in her office on Friday, just catching up. If you'd like to call her in the morning between around 9:30 and 10 a.m. PST, I can let her know you'll be calling her."

Smart Seller: "Perfect, I will call her at that time. If you have another minute, can you share with me some key training initiatives she's working on right now?"

Beth: "Well, ever since we started our new quarter, our new hires need a lot more focus because we're bringing another thirty in before the end of the year. That's one of the projects I'm working on right now."

It just took a little friendly conversation with Beth to dig out a very important—and time-saving—nugget: Ingrid is the power buyer. Compared to her, *everyone* else is a No-Po. Without this knowledge, the rep might have continued to try and reach John—who no longer works at the company, but still has a voice mail box—or Julie and Tom; or Lisa, believing her to be equal in power to Ingrid.

Make Your Contribution to the Power Buyer Clear

If you believe you don't have much to offer, or that you really don't belong at the power buyer level, you must adjust your mental focus and prepare your messaging package to meet them at that level. The higher you go up the corporate ladder, the less price resistance and competition you will meet. C-level players don't care about the features, benefits, bits, and bytes of your solution. They want to hear about business and organization issues, not product, service, or support issues. And they're always interested in the bottom line: How will your solution impact their entire organization? What profitable contribution will it make?

For example, let's say you're selling a sales training solution for a five thousand-person organization. Save the program, curriculum, costs, design, and development details for later. Instead, talk about how this training will position them ahead of their competition—within weeks of training two hundred salespeople—and how their closing ratio will increase, and how this will help the C-level with great forecasting accuracy when reporting their revenue numbers to the board.

Learn to Talk Up the Pain Chain

We have established the importance of matching your language with the different power players. Before you make the call, mentally adjust your dialogue and word choice to match three basic levels of influence:

> - Lowest = administrative
> - Middle = management
> - Highest = executive

Imagine that you are selling a complex solution involving a committee of three decision makers. They work for a two-thousand-person organization, a large manufacturing firm. This committee consists of a president/CEO, director of IT, and network administrator. Each of them has unique issues that keep them up at night. The qualities of each look like this:

The CEO/president is at the executive level:

> *Titles:* CEO, CFO, CTO, CMO, COO

> *Hot buttons:* corporate strategy, profitability, shareholders and boards, gaining market share, prestige, reputation, company viability

> *Language/buzzwords:* Raise revenues, boost visibility, stronger ROI, increase productivity, build brand loyalty, lower cost of sale

> *Sample questions:*

"What short-term goals will your company implement in order to maintain market share?"

"How have economic conditions affected information in the company?"

"What are the major issues facing your company in the next year?"

"How have recent industry trends affected your company?"

"Which markets/products do you see becoming most profitable?"

"What is going to fuel your growth over the next few years?"

The director of IT is at the management level:

> *Titles:* IS manager, marketing manager, sales manager

> *Hot buttons:* sales goals, customer satisfaction, labor costs, efficiently managing teams

> *Language/buzzwords:* increased revenues, customer retention, productive workforce, efficiently managing teams, functionality, streamlining processes

> *Sample questions:*

"How many people are currently supporting your network?"

"What are your training requirements/needs/goals/expectations?"

"What type of on-site support do you have established to manage and maintain your customer and billing records?"

"Who determines and implements your customer satisfaction goals?"

"Describe the perfect solution."

The network administrator is at the operations level:
> *Titles:* network analyst, project coordinator
> *Hot buttons:* ease of use, install, implementation, fast, seamless, intuitive, low maintenance
> *Language/buzzwords:* ease of use, fast, seamless implementation, 24/7 support, quality solution
> *Sample questions:*
>> "Tell me about the type of technology you've used in the past. What worked and what did not?"
>> "How are you currently managing your data, and what are your future plans?"
>> "What type of complaints do you receive on a daily basis from your end-users?"
>> "What type of software do you currently have in place?"
>> "What type of platforms are you running on?"

GIVING YOURSELF ACCESS: YOU DESERVE TO SPEAK WITH THE POWER BUYER!

At the beginning of this chapter, we listed some fears that keep reps from calling at the highest level within an organization. They may be loyal to their No-Po, they may lack the skill to get past the gatekeepers, and they may not have done their homework. But sometimes, it's a matter of feeling powerless yourself. In this case, the gatekeeper who's really standing between you and the power player is yourself. If you don't feel in your heart that you really *deserve* to speak with the power buyer, or that you belong in the same room with the power buyer, or have every right to be heard, all of your good intentions will get you nowhere. This chapter focuses on meeting power with power—your own. And this is the key to linking with those who wield authority.

The Power Game

In my training sessions, we play the following game that makes it very clear whether or not a person is comfortable speaking to power. I tape index cards labeled with various corporate positions—janitor, consultant, receptionist, marketing manager, technical support director, HR director, CEO, administrator, and so on—on each participant's back. I tell them that they will not know their own title, but will be able to see everyone else's title. They will then circulate around the room, meeting and greeting people according to their titles, but without directly telling the person they are talking to who that person is supposed to be. (For example, they can't say, "Oh, it's great to meet the IT director!") When everyone has met everyone else, I ask them to line up against the wall where they think they rank in the hierarchy, from CEO to janitor. They guess based on the way others responded to them. The person who had the receptionist title always says how friendly people were to them, and how much they had to talk about, but the CEO is usually alone, approached by just a few or no one.

Why is this the case? Why do we so easily choose to relinquish our power to those with big titles? Why are we intimidated, fearful, and self-conscious when approaching the highest level?

Reclaim Your Power Now!

In many ways, it's not surprising that so many people find it difficult to feel powerful. Daily life often undermines our sense of personal power in ways we are not even aware of. We can barely read the front page of the newspaper or watch the first four minutes of a television news broadcast before we get hit with accounts of forces beyond our control—from earthquakes, to fires, to drive-by shootings, to terrorist attacks—which can easily drain our sense of power. In the corporate business climate, it seems easier to relinquish power to those who hold important titles. But doing this will not give you more power, or help you feel comfortable linking with influential and powerful people.

Reclaiming your power starts with you: no one else will grant it to you. A simple way to begin boosting your own sense of personal power is with daily sales affirmations. Use these seven affirmations to help you reframe your image of yourself before you start calling power buyers:

1. I deserve to talk with C-level executives, VPs, and directors.
2. I will not allow anyone to diminish my power or self-esteem.
3. I cannot get intimidated by calling high; I have something to offer.
4. I can bring value to an organization and want to gain mindshare at the highest levels.
5. I will not accept "no" from people who have no power to say "yes."
6. I will schedule two lunch meetings per month with a personal friend or colleague who holds a high level of influence in her social or professional standing.
7. I will approach authority figures with genuine curiosity and think in terms of creating success in every situation.
8. I will continue to position myself at the highest level and feel I am important, significant, and relevant.

Cubicle Chronicles

—————— **Where's the Power in My Pipeline? Reality Check**——————

Now that you've learned how to distinguish between the powerless and the powerful, and link with them effectively, you can take another look at your sales forecast. Your sales forecast represents your qualified opportunities and estimates their probability of closing. Once you've let go of your No-Po's, you can flush the powerless out of your pipeline and make your forecast as accurate as possible.

Power-Seeker Lucy: *"I know that I shouldn't hang out with a No-Po for very long, but I was wondering . . . couldn't they actually become a power buyer at some point and make my commitment worth it?"*

Reality Check: No-Po's rarely become power buyers because they lack some of the influential qualities required to become one. Don't hang on to false hope. Once a No-Po, always a No-Po.

Power-Seeker Roger: *"My power buyer answered the phone once and gave me a few minutes of their time. He asked me to get in touch* *with his team, and I haven't been able to get him back. What am I doing wrong?"*

Reality Check: It could be that when you first spoke with him, you didn't create enough value for him to think you can help with his business. That's okay, there's still time to outline everything you know and go back to him.

Power-Seeker Lyla: *"My field partner asked me to set appointments with all C-level individuals for a call campaign. I spent weeks on it and haven't been able to reach any of them."*

Reality Check: That's not a surprise. Have you tried working with their assistants or secretaries? Have you done some homework about their company and approached them with your knowledge? Have you created value to answer their questions about why it would be worth their time to meet with your field partner?

Power-Seeker Matthew: *"I'm not sure I've identified the power buyer. I think I may be getting close, but don't understand the signals."*

Reality Check: Call around, up and down, and wide on the org chart. If all the names you get point to the same person, then you've hit the power buyer.

Power-Seeker Sasha: *"I give up! I've been trying to get in touch with this CTO for months. I've tried everything—calling his assistant, his managers, and even the department secretary. They all tell me he is extremely busy. They take my message and tell me he will get back to me, but I just don't buy it."*

Reality Check: It's time to revisit what you are saying and the messages you are leaving. How are you engaging those around him? What value are you bringing? What do your e-mails say that creates value?

LINKING STRATEGIES

1. Pay attention to the ways you may be sabotaging yourself, then ask yourself why you are so uncomfortable calling high.

2. Remember that today's power buyers are the thought leaders, the mavericks, and the high influencers, not the traditional conservative authority figures.

3. Learn how to recognize, manage, increase, and use your own level of influence.

4. Don't get fooled by big titles. Study and navigate org charts to discover the hidden sources of power.

5. Learn how to recognize power buyer e-mails and habits throughout the sales cycle.

6. Remember that executive assistants can be your doorway to finding and reaching power buyers.

7. If you want to belong at C-level, you must learn to live and breathe their world.

8. The language that works with power buyers focuses on the bottom-line contribution you bring to their organization rather than how your product or service works.

9. Learn the language that resides with various low, medium, and high levels of influence, and match that language in your phone calls. If you call high and talk low, you'll be shut out quickly.

10. It's time to reclaim your power: believe you belong and have every right to be talking with power buyers. Practice your daily sales affirmations.

CHAPTER 7

PRESENTING

It's Showtime!

Beware complexifiers and complicators.
(Truly "smart people" . . . simplify things.)

—**Tom Peters**

In this chapter, you'll get valuable insight into:

- ⊘ Why it's time inside salespeople take presentations seriously
- ⊘ Why your prospects are bailing from "death by PowerPoint"
- ⊘ How important it is to know the committee of multiple decision makers intimately
- ⊘ Why you really do need to spend up to six hours preparing for a fifteen-minute presentation

You'll learn tools and tactics to help you:

- ⊘ Design and deliver effective online, web, and video demos and presentations
- ⊘ Select PowerPoint slides that help you sell
- ⊘ Succinctly educate, motivate, and influence others about your product or service
- ⊘ Create trial closing questions that move the presentation along
- ⊘ Articulate the competitive advantages of your product/service

"Hello, everyone. We are still waiting for a few people to join us. Who just joined us? Hi Susan. Are you able to get on the conference tool? Sure, it's easy to just download the application—it will take a few minutes. John, thanks for joining us. Where are you calling from? Oh, I'm sorry your laptop just froze. You still have time to reboot while we wait for a few more people. Let me check in with who has dialed in so far. There are four people on this call and eight people have accepted invitations for this meeting. There's a loud buzz on the line . . . if everyone can press their mute button, we won't hear the feedback or the dog barking in the background. Now, that's better. John, are you still with us? Have you tried rebooting your system? Let me send you the link to log back in. Thanks for waiting, everyone. We're going to start in a few more minutes. I'm showing here that Ron, Frances, Kim, and Debbie are going to join us on this call. Is that still the case? Oh, my mobile is ringing . . . Kim is stuck in traffic and can't access the conference bridge but still wants to be on this call. Hello, who just joined us? Ron, do you know if Frances and Debbie will be joining us? Oh, good, you've got Debbie in the office with you. Welcome, Debbie! Thanks for your patience, I've got Ron, Debbie, John, Susan, Stuart, and Kim on this call. Can we begin our meeting? Good.

"I have a few slides I want to share with you today, and I've invited my systems engineer and my regional sales manager to join us for this call. I want to be respectful of time, and since we are starting at seven minutes past the hour, does everyone have a hard stop at 2 p.m. today? Sure, I understand you all have an unexpected all-hands meeting you must attend. We'll cut it down and end this meeting at half-past one. I have prepared about 120 slides that I'd like to quickly run through, and also open up a few minutes for Q&A. How does that sound?

TAKING PRESENTATIONS SERIOUSLY

Sooner or later, most sales reps find themselves stuck in presenting hell, experiencing a slow "death by PowerPoint" presentation. It's bad enough when you're just sitting through it, but when you're the one in charge of a bad presentation, and you have to keep going while you watch your prospects mentally check out, you can't help but wonder, "What happened?"

Presenting shows up late in the sales cycle, after your introducing, navigating, questioning, and linking skills have helped you move a person with the power to buy to a place where you can make a convincing and compelling pitch. It is the single biggest event that will determine if the sale has any potential of closing. You finally have them in a place where they are receptive to being educated, convinced, persuaded, and motivated to purchase your product/service offerings. This is your chance to shine, to show your prospects your knowledge of your company, your product, your competitive advantage, and their financial investment in your solution. It's also your opportunity to demonstrate what you have learned about them, to deliver new ideas, and to align your offerings to their needs. You have a captive audience waiting to be convinced.

Unfortunately, if you are like so many inside salespeople, you are woefully unprepared to give a presentation that sells your product or service the way it deserves to be sold.

Presenting is a vital skill, but one that most inside salespeople either never learn or don't take seriously. Historically, it's been a skill reserved for field sales visits. Inside sales reps have been too busy generating leads, scheduling appointments, generating quotes, responding to proposal requests, inviting prospects to demos and webinars, and hanging out on the sidelines watching their sales engineers or field partners bore their unqualified prospects to death. It's time for inside sales to drive these presentations, riding the momentum of this very critical part of the sales cycle and bringing it to closing.

Take a hard look at your presentation skills: this is fast becoming the critical point that keeps the sales cycle moving. As you learned in Chapter 2, "Introducing," it's important to create multiple "touch points" throughout the sales cycle that educate and offer value. In the beginning, these are e-mails and phone calls. As you progress through the sales cycle, webinars and demos become important touch points that have a high chance of converting to a sale. In fact, CSO Insights' 2008 "Inside Telesales Performance Optimization" report found that online demos and presentations shorten the sales cycle significantly. They note three core objectives that must be satisfied in a presentation:

1. Get prospects to understand the benefits of your solution
2. Differentiate yourself from your competition
3. Understand how they buy

In this chapter, we'll review the basic how-tos of presenting, whether you are preparing for a five-minute meeting or a thirty-minute web demo. More important, however, we will go into depth on presenting secrets: *why* you should incorporate presentations into your sales tool kit and what *not* to do. You'll learn why so many of today's prospects bail at the last minute, or butcher your time by requesting less time. You'll learn what it takes to make your presentation memorable and to propel your sales cycle forward. And you'll learn how to gather your knowledge, skills, and confidence to educate, motivate, and influence prospects when it's show time!

IT'S SALES 2.0: ALL I'VE GOT IS FOUR MINUTES!

The question "Should we schedule a web conference?" has become the new password for progressing through the sales cycle and putting people together. The online conferencing service WebEx recently sponsored a 2008 survey conducted by CXO Media on collaboration efforts. They found that 56 percent of respondents strongly agreed that on-demand collaboration tools will accelerate business, and that more than 70 percent of respondents use or will use collaboration tools to interact with customers and clients in the next twelve months.

Sales 2.0 isn't about drinking web collaboration Kool-Aid. We already know that collaboration tools have become an integral part of day-to-day interactions, and collaboration software has emerged as a key component in today's arsenal of sales communication tools. So yes, you probably should schedule a web conference. But when you do so, you need to consider your needs and your prospect's needs.

Hold That Pose

Salespeople in a Sales 2.0 landscape face these recurring and constant dilemmas: how to best reach prospects who have very little time, and how to choose the best presentation tool from an abundance of options. The biggest issue here is the fact that other people are simply clawing at the door to present!

With time in such short supply, fewer face-to-face meetings are being granted. Salespeople not only have competition from competing firms, but from individuals in their own companies who want their own chances to present online. The technical systems engineer wants to run the demo and recommend configuration and install issues. The marketing products manager wants to deliver a webinar and explain the company and how it is positioned in the market. The field sales reps' travel budgets are being scrutinized, and their prospects don't want to meet on-site. The lead generation rep needs to present to anything that moves.

So where does that leave inside salespeople? If the inside salesperson's job is to grow the opportunity and manage it along the way, it's time to step in and take control.

Why Your Prospects Bail

It's a no-brainer to predict that many of your prospects will bail from webinars, will request shorter presentations, will insist on evaluating the demo on their own before sitting through a presentation, will cancel at the last minute, or will inform you they only have fifteen minutes and want to see four to six slides max.

Can you blame them? Think about it. If a sales rep is averaging between three and five technical demos per week, and fewer decision makers are granting face-to-face meetings, then it is safe to assume that decision makers are sitting through a few *dozen* online presentations per week. There should be a rapid rewards club for PowerPoint viewers, because these prospects are averaging one thousand slides viewed weekly! A white paper sponsored by GoToMeeting entitled "How to Create an On-Demand Webinar Program" surveyed organizations holding regular webinars and discovered that over 52 percent of these webinars are recorded every time. These on-demand webinars extend the life cycle of the webinar.

It's time for inside sales reps to stop abusing their presentation privileges with prospects. We've been so busy rocking customers to sleep with these "death by PowerPoint" presentations that we've forgotten about their needs. What do they really want to see, touch, hear, feel, and think? They have been fed too many features and benefits and now are hungry for real value. We've been so busy manipulating metrics and getting anyone who says "yes" to attend a demo that we didn't take the time to evaluate *who* would be showing up and how much of their time we would be soaking up. We've delayed our qualification efforts, thrown No-Po's into a demo, and then listened to them create wish lists that they will never afford. We continue to recycle old slides and deliver substandard presentations and hope to close a deal. In a Sales 2.0 world, there is even less room for mistakes than there used to be.

Think about it: Would *you* buy something that was presented in this way?

Remember the Sales 2.0 reality mantra: "I can give you four minutes." In those four minutes, prospects want to hear a strong value prop, a compelling competitive advantage story, and a well-calculated ROI (return on investment) that makes them look like a hero. You might then earn more time if you have piqued their interest with the initial presentation.

If all the work you've done with the client so far is going to pay off, then those four minutes have to count. And for those four minutes to count, you need to take them seriously, do your homework, and give a presentation the prospect will remember. Keep your prospect's needs in the front of your mind, make sure they're met in a memorable way, and don't forget to record the session, in case half of the committee doesn't show up!

UNDERSTAND THE PROCESS

Most presentation training focuses on face-to-face presentations. Participants learn about eye contact, posture, and the best way to work the remote for their slides. They watch their videotape for feedback, and then often leave completely unprepared to handle a web or video conference or webinar. If they received training on web demos, it's focused around how to use the tool, adjust their web cam, and turn the "record" switch on.

If you're feeling unprepared to host a presentation, the first step you might take is to do a Google search for a list of rules to follow. The good news is, you won't have any trouble finding them. The bad news is, there are tons of presentation rules out there and you can become lost and confused very quickly. Is it really important which font you use on your PowerPoint slides, how to create fancy builds and design compelling pie charts?

Not so much. It's much more important to create a presentation that showcases your product or service, that emphasizes your confidence in it, that speaks to your prospect's needs, that does not waste their time, and that holds their interest in a compelling way that moves the deal to closing.

That's why a much better approach to honing your presenting skills is taking the time—yes, your precious time—to understand the entire process: the content, the prep time, and the presentation itself. When you have mastered these components, putting together presentations will be much easier, and much more effective than you ever thought possible.

Quick Preparation Checklist for Your Presentation

Once you've determined the type of presentation you are making, prep time is vital! It includes everything from researching the people who will attend the presentation, to organizing your content, to rehearsing and timing your delivery. Whether your presentation is fifteen minutes or two hours and fifteen minutes, the same amount of preparation must happen. Here's a preparation checklist for a fifteen-minute presentation:

- ⦿ Qualify the prospect (30 minutes)
- ⦿ Conduct needs assessment before your presentation to learn who will be attending and what their needs will be (30 minutes)
- ⦿ Review your qualification criteria to confirm the needs you gathered (15 minutes)
- ⦿ Send invitations and reminders (15 minutes)
- ⦿ Prepare and design slides (one hour)
- ⦿ Rehearse and practice (one hour)

Yes, that's a total of 3.5 hours of planning for a finely tuned and well-executed fifteen-minute presentation. This pays off when you can move the deal forward.

CHOOSE THE RIGHT PRESENTATION TYPE

Today, presentations can be made right from your desktop. CSO Insights' "Improving Inside Sales Effectiveness Using Technology" report found that companies who did online demos and webinars had a quota attainment of 63 percent. They also found that the higher the deal size, the more online collaboration tools were used.

You must have a good variety of presentations in your bag of tricks, and you must also be aware of which type is suitable for which audience. Get to know your audience or committee members in terms of functional responsibilities, their experience, and their level of influence. They most often fall into one of the following categories:

1. Technical buyer who is responsible for the technical due diligence of the project
2. Economic or business buyer who is responsible for the financial aspects of the project
3. End-user buyer who will be utilizing your product or service
4. Coach or informant who will guide you and give you information

It may seem obvious that a technical proof-of-concept demo is very different from a general high-level presentation, or that presentations should be very different in different parts of the sales cycle, or that you don't want to give the same presentation to the same people more than once, but the novice can easily overlook these kinds of details.

Let's explore the various types of presentation choices, the target audiences, and timing in the sales cycle.

Webinar

These web seminars are free to attend and can be viewed live or on-demand later, via a specific web link. They generally last about thirty to fifty-five minutes, and are generally delivered by the marketing organization. They usually provide a high-level overview of the company and product, and a speaker may be invited.

Participants may submit questions, or even interact with other participants. The content may be fairly general and focused around a popular topic geared to drive interest. The statistics on users who download the on-demand webinar up to twelve months after the recording are high. Webinars are generally attended by lower-level, technical, and end-user influencers and recommenders. These attendees don't necessarily manage a budget, but they are the ones who need to become educated on the product.

The webinar is effective early in the sales cycle, during the qualification efforts illustrated in Chapter 4, "Questioning." In addition, it gives your prospects an opportunity to qualify themselves. The webinar might also be used with existing customers who want to view new product releases.

Technical Demo and Evaluation

A technical demo is delivered through a web collaboration tool. It provides the prospect with a technical demo of the project based on the client's current environment. This is common in large enterprise and consultative selling environments where configuration issues must be discussed. These demos are known to be fairly long, lasting up to seventy-five minutes.

A technical systems engineer plays a major role in managing this kind of demo, spending time explaining configuration, installation, and adoption issues concerning how the product or service will fit into the prospect's environment. The prospect may want to know more about your competitive advantage. The end-user and technical influencer are usually part of this session, but watch out—this person may be a recommender or a No-Po. Be careful! No-Po's are usually technically astute and ask all the right questions. As mentioned in Chapter 3, "Navigating," they may also bring their entourage to your presentation. Keep in mind that if they are No-Po's, you can invest time educating and using them to extract more key information since they are willing to give you time. In fact, they will give you *lots* of time because they have lots of questions. Just remember not to stop the process here—they will never make a purchase decision.

This demo is recommended in the middle of the sales cycle, after you've qualified the prospect and can dedicate your technical resources to a technical demo and evaluation.

Business Presentation

A business presentation may be delivered through a web or video conference tool. It must be short—not more than fifteen or twenty minutes.

This kind of presentation must be customized and delivered from a high-level business perspective, and the participants should include the economic or business influencer. The inside rep or field or sales manager must drive this presentation because it includes business reasons for purchasing your product. Remember, this presentation is for the power buyers—people with very little time to give you. They will want to know key benefits of your solution, value propositions, and competitive advantage.

Remember, too, that the business presentation happens *only* after the qualification and technical discussion has taken place.

Proof-of-Concept/ROI Business Presentation

This presentation is delivered farther along in the sales cycle, after the technical and business issues have been addressed.

This short presentation must focus on the financial investment and the hard business reasons for justifying the purchase of your product in the short and long term. It must be very short—no more than fifteen minutes. Your prospects will also want to know the proposed competitive advantage and ROI (return on investment). The participants must be economic influencers who manage the budget. It's the power buyer and the economic influencer who need convincing.

KNOW WHO'S DRIVING

Guess what? *You* are driving the presentation—*regardless of who will be participating in the demo!* Never give up control when it's your deal on the table. You may allow others to be involved as long as you control their time and set expectations with your prospects.

Sometimes, inevitably, someone other than you will be in control. When everyone in the company wants to be part of the performance, they tend to bring their own agendas and forget about the customer. It's common for inside salespeople to take the back seat in most presentations because they may not feel technically proficient and believe their systems engineers will do a better job. Be present 100 percent of the time. Don't cheat yourself or your prospects—you're the one that got them there!

Get to Know Your Committee Intimately

Don't lose sight of your audience, the end-users of your presentation. Remember, most decisions are made by committee by this point in the sales cycle, and you should have gotten to know your committee members intimately. Some questions to think about would be: *"What are their backgrounds? What are they looking for—concrete information, concepts, theory? What are their expectations? How will they buy?"* This will allow you to customize a stronger presentation for them, and it's the perfect foundation for presenting.

Once you've answered these questions, you can bet that what's running through each of their minds are some of the following questions and concerns you will be expected to answer:

➤ "Why should I buy your product?"
➤ "What is the hard dollar value (ROI)?"
➤ "What problems does your product or service solve?"
➤ "What will it do for my business?"
➤ "What happens if I don't buy your product?"
➤ "What if we just built an in-house solution?"
➤ "What goal will it help me realize?"
➤ "What other value is there (prestige, safety)?"
➤ "Why should I buy it now?"

Manage Logistics

Logistics involves planning how your meeting will be structured before, during, and after your presentation. Determine when you will start and end, how long the meeting will be, how your information will flow, what order your slides will be in, how you will open and how you will close, and so on. How many participants will you invite? The more participants you must manage and the more tools you will use, the more you will have to think about.

Send Invitations. Once you've decided whom to invite, send invitations. I recommend sending Outlook Meeting Requests to confirm. Include a strong subject line, such as:

[YOUR COMPANY NAME] Presents Key Findings for 2009 to [PROSPECT]

Building Solutions Discussion with [PROSPECT] on August 18, 2009

15-Minute Demo Confirmation with [PROSPECT] for August 18, 2009

Do not send the slides prior to the meeting, and remember to send a reminder twenty-four hours in advance.

When the attendees accept, send out announcements confirming their participation along with log-in instructions.

At meeting time, log in at least fifteen minutes early. Participants do not like to check into meetings on time only to discover the host has not yet shown up!

Visualize the Meeting. Sit down and go through the meeting in your mind, step by step. Visualize everything that will happen and might accidentally happen—people who are latecomers or no-shows, slides that don't work, sudden time constraints—and make sure you have everything covered.

Don't Let Technology Trip You Up

As technology and tools continue to evolve, technical issues will be inevitable—but they can also be preventable. The more you know in advance about what to expect, the better prepared you will be. For example, if you are preparing a web demo, will your committee be viewing your slides in a conference room all together, or will they be in their cubicles previewing your demo? If you are going to record the event, will your audience have audio? Video? Should you set up your web cam and check screen resolution in advance? Keep in mind that everyone has different ways of viewing your presentation, and understand the various platforms or browsers they will use.

Allow time in advance to trouble-shoot all the possible issues that may arise. If you are able to spend less time on the mechanics of the presentation, you can spend more time on the sale!

BE 100 PERCENT PRESENT WHEN PRESENTING

What you say will need to persuade the participants—which means it can't bore them, annoy them, or waste their time. It's time we all stop hiding behind our visuals, recycling tons of outdated PowerPoint slide decks. Remember: PowerPoint is not the presentation—you are. Slides are meant to support the narration of the speaker, not distract or compete with the speaker. When you're presenting, the number one most important thing is to *be present*!

The Rules

You've probably read a lot of presentation rules by now (as I have also) but I find Guy Kawasaki sums it up well in his How to Change the World Blog, which he refers to as the 10/20/30 Rules of Power-Point: ten slides/twenty minutes/thirty + font size.

Here are my ten rules, short and sweet.

1. Keep Your Fonts Simple. Use the same font set throughout your entire presentation—stay consistent. Some companies require you use certain fonts. Find a font that is professional and friendly and use it throughout. Make sure you know the difference between a serif font (like Times New Roman) and a sans-serif font (like Helvetica or Arial). The font I recommend for clarity is Gill Sans.

2. Keep the Presentation Short. Expect presentations to become shorter and shorter in the future, and plan accordingly. It's okay to have a shorter presentation, because that keeps your audience wanting more. Aim for fifteen minutes. Spend ten minutes presenting and five minutes in a question-and-answer discussion.

Organize your content on a pad of paper or on a whiteboard before you begin. Be careful not to offer a data dump. Presenters often get attached to all their content, believing that everything they have to say is important. It's not. Focus on the core of your idea or message. Strip the extra away. A good exercise is to ask yourself if your audience could remember only three things about your presentation, what would you want them to be?

3. The Best Slides Have Graphics and Very Little Text. People remember visuals more than they remember text. Don't get carried away writing too much on your slides. Think about the following:

➤ Avoid overdoing colorful graphics. It's easy to get lost in them, and they can easily distract people from your message.

➤ Use photographs. They usually engage audiences on an emotional level. Make sure they are high quality, and don't include low-resolution images.

➤ Avoid using PowerPoint clip art that your audience has seen a million times.

➤ Colors can be divided into two categories: cool (such as blue and green) and warm (such as orange and red). Cool colors work best in backgrounds and warm colors work best for objects in the foreground.

If you have to use text:

➤ Pick one simple font (such as Arial or Gill Sans) and use it consistently.

➤ Use bullet lists instead of whole paragraphs. Keep text clear, concise, and legible.

➤ If you must have text, follow the 7x7 rule: Limit the words on a visual to no more than seven words per line and a maximum of seven lines, totaling forty-nine words or less.

4. Avoid Cluttered Charts, Graphs, and Tables. Many presenters include too much data on their charts. You can choose to display your data in graphic form, such as pie charts, vertical bar charts, horizontal bar charts, or line charts. When you need to make side-by-side comparisons, use tables.

5. Organize Your Slides Ahead of Time. It's important to logically lay out what you plan on presenting. That's where the slide sorter comes in. Start by determining your goal. What are key take-away concepts?

Many organizations mandate you build your slides using their templates, but this is an area you may want to get more creative about.

I suggest a maximum of eight slides—that's it:

- ➤ Slide #1: Introduction slide. Include the client's logo on slide.
- ➤ Slide #2: Objective. What is the goal? What are you going to talk about?
- ➤ Slide #3: Agenda. Highlight what you plan on presenting.
- ➤ Slide #4: Needs uncovered. Whom you spoke with and what you uncovered.
- ➤ Slide #5: Solutions and recommendations. Highlight why your solution is the best in the market and what your competitive advantage is. Include your value proposition and benefit statements.
- ➤ Slide #6: Proof points. Customer testimonial or case study.
- ➤ Slide #7: ROI. Why you are the best investment out there.
- ➤ Slide #8: Close and next steps. Summarize needs and benefits and suggest subsequent action steps.

6. Do Not Read Your Own Slides! Why torture your prospects by reading through slides they can read themselves? Instead, use a few key words to help you explain concepts. The best way to gain, maintain, and sustain the audience's attention is to surprise them by creating interest beyond the slide. You may be the first presenter that month to do so.

7. Keep Their Attention with Interactivity. Getting and keeping someone's attention is very tough. When you are presenting to a committee, keep in mind that not only do their members have various levels of influence, but they all learn at different speeds. Individuals learn very differently and are motivated by different things.

One idea is to create interactive presentations, where you get the audience talking. Prospects learn better when they are actively participating. No audience likes being "talked at," even for a relatively short time. If you create a discussion-style presentation, it encourages participation from your audience and gives them an opportunity to learn from each other and share life and job experiences.

8. Be an Enthusiastic Communicator and Group Leader. A boring or monotone speaker just encourages the audience to lose sight of the presentation. Use enthusiasm and confidence to take the audience where you want them to go. Use the same skills you've honed for phone calls. Speak succinctly, question well, and listen actively. Don't interrupt or monopolize the conversation.

Begin with a round of introductions. Everyone should have a clear understanding of who is on the call. Explain the purpose of the meeting and set ground rules, confirm time and needs you have uncovered from participants. Use a positive story or anecdote that portrays your service and commitment. Be clear with your words and organize your thoughts to keep the meeting moving quickly and on track.

9. Ask Trial Closing Questions. Because you are dealing with an audience that is distracted, it is important throughout your presentation to check in with your participants to gain acknowledgment and cooperation. The best way to check the pulse is by asking trial closing questions every few minutes or after every couple of slides. During the presentation, you can use a softer approach; toward the end of the presentation, you can use a harder approach. Here are some examples:

Soft trial closes:
- "How does this sound to you?"
- "How do you see this fitting in within your organization?"
- "Have I accurately summarized your needs?"

Hard trial closes:

> ➤ "What is making you hesitate?"
> ➤ "Is there anything I haven't covered that you have questions about?"
> ➤ "What do you see taking place from now until then?"
> ➤ "How close are you to making a decision?"
> ➤ "Are you ready to make a decision?"
> ➤ "What do we need to do to get this done?"
> ➤ "Is there anything that would prevent you from moving forward on this proposal?"
> ➤ "Would you like to move forward on this?"
> ➤ "Are you ready to get started?"
> ➤ "What is our next step?"
> ➤ "Should I forward a contract to your purchasing department?"

10. Plan a Strong Opening and a Strong Closing. Audience attention is always highest at the beginning and closing of your presentation.

> ➤ Grab audience attention by starting with a story, asking questions, throwing out a compelling statistic—and then get to the formalities and ground rules.
> ➤ Allow time for Q&A, but do not end your presentation with this. For every forty-five minutes of content, you need to allow fifteen minutes for Q&A.
> ➤ At the end, present a summary of major points, provide time for questions, and then deliver a prepared close that is different from the summary. The prepared close is your time to provide the audience with an inspiring vision that helps them focus on what they can do with the new information you have just presented.

THINK ABOUT YOUR CONTENT

Organization is great—but you have to have something of value to organize and your message must be consistent. The content is the heart of the meeting. It's the whole reason your prospects are there. What you talk about—and what your slides are meant to illustrate— must include three vital components:

1. Your value proposition
2. The ROI
3. Tour competitive advantage

Articulate Your Value Proposition

Many salespeople suffer from value messaging paralysis—the inability to clearly articulate a value proposition in as few words as possible. This is when you get a handle on the value of your company for customers and apply it to your new prospect. Be succinct: your value proposition should be brief, memorable, and provide a solution to their pain.

When articulated well, a value proposition is memorable and branded. Here are some classic examples:

Wal-Mart—Everyday low prices

BMW—The ultimate driving machine

7-Up—The Uncola

McDonald's Consistency

Domino's pizza—Fast delivery

Google—Fast, extensive searches

Avis—We try harder

These are things to think about when designing a value proposition:

1. What is the tangible difference in a characteristic of your product or service, one that actually matters to your customers?
2. How will your company help the prospect's business? Will you help them increase revenue?
3. What is your market focus and the target audience you serve?

4. What is a tangible way you will prove and promote the value you bring?

5. What are current trends in your market?

6. What differentiates your company from competitors? Is it in lowering costs? Improving profitability? Improving quantity?

7. What external factors are affecting your business?

8. How are those external factors affecting job roles?

9. What about anticipated needs and pain points?

10. Why should the prospect choose to do business with you? Can you quantify that value?

What's the ROI?

The ability to cost-justify purchases ranked second highest as a factor needing improvement in inside sales, according to CSO Insights' 2008 Telesales Survey. As companies tighten their belts, and budgets are scrutinized, more and more projects compete for the same tight dollar pool. Your opportunity is being weighed against several other projects, and there are probably more people than ever involved in the buying decision, so that means more inputs informing this decision.

Evaluating the "return on investment" (ROI) for a prospect/customer makes it easier for him or her to justify spending money on your product or service and helps the prospect visualize the value the purchase or investment will create. Return on investment is defined as the amount of monetary value one can expect to receive as the result of making an investment. An investment is anything that is purchased for the purpose of generating income (or decreasing expenses), or an item that is expected to increase in value over time.

Your goal is to put the value your product or service creates in context for your prospect. Sales professionals create this context by breaking down the costs associated with the product or service and illustrating how the purchase or investment provides a positive rate of return for the company. This sales skill will help you position your offering apart from your competitors and ultimately make moving forward with you more compelling.

Here's a quick way to translate the ROI into terms the prospect can understand, as described by JustSell.com at http://www.justsell.com/salestools/returnoninvestment.aspx:

1. What's the direct cost of your product or service, and how much will it cost to implement?

2. What's the customer's benefit in real dollars every month—in terms of increased revenue—because of your service/product and savings on expenditures they won't have to make?

3. Multiply the benefit amount in #2 by twelve months to get the annual financial benefit, and subtract the cost of the product/service as determined in #1.

4. Now divide this number by the cost determined in #1, and multiply by 100. That's your ROI percentage.

What's Your Competitive Advantage?

What makes you better than your competition? If you don't know, your prospect is not going to care enough to work it out on their own.

CSO Insights' "2008 Inside/Telesales Performance Optimization" report confirms that there is room for improvement in the area of differentiating your offerings from the competition. It is critical for inside sales teams to not only know about who else is out there, but to also clearly articulate their competitive advantage and have a competitive strategy in place.

Cubicle Chronicles

———————————— **Presenting Reality Check**————————————

Data-Dumping Debra: *"I get so excited about explaining our product offerings that I may pitch too soon. Then feel like I've lost my prospect, who becomes fidgety and distracted. How do I reel them back in?"*

Reality Check: You are probably telling and not selling, and not engaging the customer in the process. If you spend more time engaging your audience by creating opportunities for discussion, they will listen and participate.

Last-Minute-Cancellations Carla: *"Help! I'm always scheduling presentations and then, on the day of, I get so many last-minute cancellations. Is it my bad phone breath?"*

Reality Check: As we predicted in this chapter, you must expect cancellations, but you can prevent some of them by doing the following:

1. Set clear expectations with your audience, in an e-mail format, on what they will walk away with from attending your demo or presentation.
2. Include an inviting subject line on their invitation.
3. Continue to individually massage each committee member who will be attending by sending them e-mails with new ideas as the time gets closer.
4. Remind them you will record the event and make it available for on-demand viewing.

Can't-See-the-Slides Sam: *"This always seems to happen to one of my participants who joins the demo or presentation—they don't have connectivity, so they can't see the slides. Should I send the slides beforehand?"*

Reality Check: Don't let the "no slides" issue get in your way. Instead, since you have the customer live, take the opportunity to have a discussion with the prospect on the phone and talk through three major points from your presentation. Then you can send him or her the slides or a brief e-mail recap of your discussion.

Blind-Sided Ben: *"Things were moving along fine, and then I heard chatter on the other line. Apparently, someone from the prospect's side had just joined the presentation and I had no idea who they were. They started asking all these questions and taking control."*

Reality Check: Be very careful of this! Power buyers tend to walk in late and leave early for meetings, so it could be a power buyer.

Perform a quick power biopsy. Quickly ask them to introduce themselves and explain what their role is, and listen to how the dynamics shift. If everyone becomes silent when they talk, you may want to direct more of your information in their direction.

Stuck-with-the-Geeks Greg: *"Every time I schedule our technical systems engineer for a demo, he takes over and gets so technical that I fall asleep. He seems to have little regard for salespeople and wants to talk bits and bytes. Then I feel I lose the sale completely. What can I do to take control?"*

Reality Check: Have an honest discussion with your technical engineer and help him or her understand the difference between a technical versus a business sales discussion. Limit the amount of time and slides he or she can have on the call, and make sure you're in agreement before you begin.

PRESENTING STRATEGIES

1. Presenting is a vital skill. Done well, it will turbocharge your sales cycle and get you closer to closing more business.

2. Preparing for a fifteen-minute presentation takes about the same amount of time as preparing for a ninety-minute presentation. Do your homework!

3. Your prospects are bailing from face-to-face meetings and will only give you four minutes. No problem! Decide how to maximize your time and determine what type of presentation you will choose.

4. Stop filling seats with No-Po's. Send invites to the *right* people on the committee. Make sure you have a good assortment of technical people, economic people, and end-users, and coach buyers on the call.

5. Make sure you have a good assortment of presentations throughout your sales cycle, from a webinar to a proof-of-concept demo.

6. Technology can easily get in the way of an effective presentation. Don't let this happen. Trouble-shoot all the possible things that can go wrong beforehand and prevent it from happening. If you can't prevent it, at least you'll be prepared to deal with it.

7. Don't rely on PowerPoint. Use fewer slides—a maximum of eight—and keep them simple and short. Don't insult your audience by reading each slide!

8. Trial closing questions throughout the presentation are very necessary, especially when you cannot see what your prospects are thinking.

9. Spend time on building a strong value proposition, ROI, and competitive advantage story into your presentation.

10. Look in the mirror and smile. Remember, your presentation is your baby. Stop hiding behind slides or behind other people in your company who want to take the controls.

CHAPTER 8

HANDLING OBJECTIONS

Bring Them On!

Sometimes we stare so long at a door that is closing that we see too late the one that is open.

—Alexander Graham Bell

In this chapter, you'll get valuable insight into:

- ⊘ The objection tidal wave and how to avoid it
- ⊘ How you may actually be creating objections
- ⊘ Pitfalls of fearing rejection and taking objections personally
- ⊘ The motivational traps we fall into

You'll learn tools and tactics to help you:

- ⊘ Understand the barriers you create and how resistance keeps you down
- ⊘ Understand common reasons that customers resist
- ⊘ Differentiate between spoken and silent objections
- ⊘ Recognize warning signs that your sales may be in danger
- ⊘ Understand why your prospect goes radio silent on you
- ⊘ Understand e-mail objections and how to rebut them
- ⊘ Arm yourself with the Comeback Pack—one hundred rebuttal solutions

"I don't have time to talk."

"I'm NOT interested."

"I don't have any needs at this time."

"We're just looking."

"We're already using a competitive product."

"My boss does not want us to pursue this."

"Your service/product is too complicated."

"Send me some information and I will review it when I have time."

"You're too expensive."

"It's not in our budget."

"We'll get back to you once we have a better idea of our initiative."

"Give me a call back in Q1."

"Looks like we'll put this aside and revisit it next year."

"We'll have a new team in place so let's connect after the holidays."

"There's too much going on right now, let's talk early next year."

"Our budget is set for the rest of the year."

"We'll know more about our needs in the next few months."

These are the usual responses I receive in my training classes when I have everyone write down the most common objection phrases they receive each day.

THE BRUTAL TRUTH ABOUT OBJECTIONS

The brutal truth is that, if you find yourself fielding a torrent of customer objections and losing prospects right and left, the problem may not be your product or service. Your approach may actually be *creating* objections. It's time to take a step back and analyze what lies behind these objections. Why do you get them? From whom do you get them? When in the sales cycle do they come up? What skills do you need to acquire to handle them next time?

Some objections, of course, may have nothing to do with you. What you *are* responsible for is handling the objection in a way that not only defuses it but opens the door to more discussion. All too often, salespeople give up too soon, or lack the skills to understand what they did wrong, or are afraid to ask because they are afraid of the answer. That stops now!

CSO Insights' 2008 Inside/Telesales Performance Optimization Survey of five hundred companies found that the primary reasons salespeople win deals are service and relationships, not product superiority. Almost half—47.5 percent—of the companies surveyed admit they need improvement in understanding why they lose deals.

This sad state of affairs was confirmed by Miller Heiman's 2008 Best Practices Study, which found that fewer than 26 percent of salespeople follow up after they have lost a sale to understand their "win or lose" criteria. "It's not easy to ask someone who rejected you for feedback," they say, "but it is worth pursuing." This may seem counterintuitive, but there is no better time to learn from a mistake than right after you've made it. Call back and ask for an honest answer: Why did you lose the deal? Not only is this good for your credibility and professionalism, the answer will help you learn to improve your game.

As we'll see, there are many reasons for customers to raise objections, and not all of them are your responsibility. But the odds are that if you find yourself fielding objection after objection, you could use some attitude and skill building! This chapter begins by looking at how Sales 2.0 creates even more objections than you may be used to receiving, including five ways to ride out this tidal wave. It then looks at how salespeople create objection, and examines strategies for breaking through your own resistance to selling. It also explains why customers object, and identifies five major categories of customer objections so that you can gain the confidence and skills to rebound and overcome them.

Finally, you'll take away a highly effective tool—an objection survival guide for tough times that you can use over and over again. The *Comeback Pack* is a set of one hundred rebuttal questions, phrases, and comebacks to build up your flex power and keep you bouncing back every time.

Warning Signs Your Sale May Be in Danger

There should be no lulls in a sales cycle. If there are, you are risking rejection. You need to constantly stay on guard and continue to provide value along the way. The following warning signs are clues that your sale may be in danger:

> - Your prospect is not returning your calls or e-mails.
> - Your prospect seems to be stepping into a meeting every time you get him or her live on the phone.
> - Your prospect has stopped providing you with updates.
> - Your prospect is requesting information to help them either better "sell" your service or "compare" your service to the competition.
> - Your prospect is putting you off and coming up with new excuses for needing budget approval.
> - Your prospect assures you they are the main contact and discourages you from contacting his or her boss.
> - Your prospect is talking with the competition.

RIDING THE OBJECTION TIDAL WAVE IN SALES 2.0

Sales 2.0 is part of a volatile economy—which means you can expect *more* of everything: more excuses, higher quotas, more competitors—and more objections. These objections will come via e-mail, phone, text, or silence, and they will not be sugarcoated—few people have time to spare your feelings.

Brace yourself for a bumpy ride, especially if you honed your skills during a high point in the economic cycle, when everyone was buying and few were objecting! It's not going to be easy, but you can ride this wave—if you're prepared. Even companies that are dealing with uncertainty must still purchase goods and services to survive. Your solutions to their problems will still answer their pain. And, as always, it's still your job to convince them—with your own Sales 2.0 stimulus package that increases hope and demand.

Five Ways to Ride Out the Objection Tidal Wave

1. Replace the time you might spend panicking by working smarter and utilizing your sales tools.
2. Be efficient in everything you do—your meetings, your writing, your prospecting efforts, and even your friendships.
3. Prepare a Plan B. What's next? And after that? Don't let yourself get blindsided again.
4. ROI doesn't stand for running out of income, it stands for return on investment! Your prospects are very risk-adverse now, so create a reason for them to buy and make them heroes for their sound investment in your solution.
5. Pump up your listening. This is a time when customers want to feel heard and listened to. They don't want you to tell them what they need—even if your recommendations are right.

HOW SALESPEOPLE CREATE OBJECTIONS

Salespeople make a phenomenal number of outbound calls and send more e-mails every day and every week, and risk being rejected 99 percent of the time. A good salesperson anticipates objections and works at preventing them from coming up. But a salesperson who lacks awareness of their skill level in this regard may actually contribute to creating the objections they receive.

The phone is a transparent tool. Your confidence and drive are demonstrated in your voice. For example, if you are feeling negative or unsure about your product or service, your attitude and tone may be setting the stage for a similar response. If you lack confidence in yourself or your solution, so will the prospect—even if everything you are saying is positive.

Becoming more aware of what you may be doing to create objections will help minimize them. Most salespeople tend to be extroverts, reaching out to others. But if we want to understand what our role is in creating objections, we need to look inward. Take a minute to think about it: When you receive an objection, do you take it personally? Do you listen to what is behind the objection instead of reacting or just hanging up? Are your fears of being rejected actually helping you *create* most of the objections you receive? What keeps you from bouncing back with a response that may help your prospects change their minds?

One or more of five key problem areas—lack of sales skills, poor self-image, negative self-talk, fear of rejection, and falling into motivational traps—may be contributing to the creation of sales objections. Let's take a closer look.

Lack of Sales Skills

Lack of good product, process, and sales skills is typical of new hires that are shown their cubicle and their phone and told to get out there and sell—with little or no training to help them do it. These new hires may lack skills in prioritizing their calls, having a strong opening statement, talking with the right person, asking enough questions, or listening for the answer, as well as in presenting and closing.

The solution is to sharpen skills in any way possible. Write down what you need to learn about your products, services, and industry. Identify strategies for gaining this knowledge, even if it is just asking a supervisor or a colleague a few carefully worded questions. Take an inventory of the areas you are weak in and find mentors to help you develop. Take the initiative to get the help you need in order to build your confidence. There is nothing holding you back except yourself.

Poor Self-Image

Do you see yourself as an expert in your field? A bearer of good news? A problem solver? Unless you answered an unqualified "yes" to all three questions, you're approaching prospects timidly and tentatively.

Your self-image serves or attacks your self-esteem. Do everything you can to build yourself up, not tear yourself down. Remember that the telephone transmits everything!

Negative Self-Talk

Negative thinkers say negative things to themselves all day long:

"I don't think I'm cut out for sales."

"I sound like a broken record. Nobody wants to hear about this."

"I'm just bugging these people. They are busy. I should leave them alone."

This kind of talk holds you down, and the negativity is automatically transmitted to your prospect.

Listen to what you're telling yourself. If you hear a negative thought, stop! Instead, substitute a positive or encouraging thought, such as:

"It's their job to learn about my solution. The only way to stimulate a bad economy is when somebody buys something."

"My timing is perfect for this solution."

"He will enjoy my call more than anyone else this morning."

Whatever you are thinking is what the customer will hear.

Fear of Rejection

Some salespeople resist the sale as much or even more than the customer. The number one reason is fear of rejection. If the prospect says "no" immediately, then the salesperson never has to get to the brink of a sale, only to be rejected. Ironically, the objections they hear actually contribute to the objection they receive.

Here's another phrase I often hear from salespeople who fear rejection: *"You sound busy, so I'll let you go."* I have a pet peeve about this phrase. Quite frankly, I believe it's a cop-out. The salesperson is really saying something else entirely:

> ➤ "I really want to go, but I'll make it sound like you really want to go."
> ➤ "I don't have much more to say so I'll cut this short."
> ➤ "I fear rejection so I'll just make it easy on everyone here."

When a person operates out of a fear of rejection, they end up pushing prospects, friends, and family away. When they push them away, they create the rejection and the cycle continues. If you fear rejection, sales may be the wrong profession for you. If you are determined to stay in sales, dig deep to understand what is driving your behavior or feelings. You may want to consider counseling to help you better understand yourself.

Falling into Motivational Traps

Fear of rejection can wear down your motivation. Many salespeople make these motivational mistakes and wonder why they are getting burned out and losing their drive. Make sure to not fall into these five motivational traps:

1. *External focus.* You blame your territory, manager, product, or time of year for your objections. It's easy to look outside of yourself for what isn't working instead of doing more introspective work about your values and your goals.

2. *Comfort zone.* It's so easy to hang out with our default position—even if it's not working—instead of stretching ourselves. Shake things up, try something new. More than likely, you'll get better results.

3. *The quick fix.* Stop looking for low-hanging fruit and do the work that makes things happen. Take a step back and design a strategy, roadmap, and plan.

4. *Happy ears.* As mentioned when we discussed the listening skill, when we live in a world created by our assumptions, our perceptions never align with reality. Listen to what's really being said.

5. *Still waiting.* What are you waiting for? If you don't motivate yourself, no one else will do it for you. Decide on your top three priorities and make them happen *now*.

How to Make Them Say "No" at Every Point in the Sales Cycle

If you think you're not the source of the objections you've been getting lately, think again. It's entirely possible—and very, very common—for salespeople to unwittingly cause prospects to say "no" at every step in the sales cycle. Review the following objection triggers, and stop doing them now!

Before the call:

> Blaming the company, the management, or the product for the objections you receive

> Underestimating how important your product or service may be to the customer's business

> Not properly researching the target company

At the beginning of the call:

> Not establishing rapport

> Not sounding confident or knowledgeable

> Asking sensitive questions too soon

When qualifying:

> Qualifying on timeframe and budget only

> Not establishing the caller's role in the decision-making process

When questioning:

> Assuming your prospect's needs instead of asking about them

> Asking questions in the wrong order

> Asking for information without giving them information in return

> Not probing deep enough

When listening:

> Failing to listen for the customer's real needs

> Spending time arguing instead of listening

> Taking objections personally

When positioning:

> ➤ Not targeting the product or service to the customer's position and interests
> ➤ Trying to please everyone: making the product or service sound too good to be true
> ➤ Not presenting the benefits the customer needs or presenting the benefits of a product the customer doesn't need
> ➤ Not being persuasive: underplaying the offer

WHY CUSTOMERS OBJECT

Good news: It's not all your fault! Customers have their own reasons for saying no, and they may have little or nothing to do with you. Here are ten good reasons why customers object:

1. They're really not a match for your service or product.
2. They don't understand what you're telling them.
3. They don't believe what you're telling them.
4. They think there might be problems down the road if they buy your product.
5. There really *are* problems with buying your product.
6. They're No-Po's—they're not authorized to make purchasing decisions.
7. They're afraid of you.
8. They're afraid of change.
9. They have been programmed for disaster by bad experiences, and saying "no" is their best defense.
10. They're not sold yet.

Types of Objections

Today's sales cycle is larger and lasts longer then it used to. It affects more people, their work, their performance, and their results. People can be anxious about making purchasing decisions when the cost of a mistake—including time, money, lost productivity, and even criticism—is so great. The objections you'll receive will come in various guises. It's a good idea to be aware of all of them.

The Unspoken Objection. The unspoken objection is not voiced by the prospect. In many ways, it is probably the most dangerous objection to handle because the telephone makes it difficult to read an unspoken objection. For example, the prospect may say, "*I just don't have the time,*" when what they really mean is they don't like calls from vendors, they don't take women who sell technology seriously, or that they think your accent makes it sound as though your service has been outsourced.

The False Objection. The false objection is an argument or excuse offered by the prospect in an effort to resist a pitch or to delay making a decision—all in a way that avoids the unpleasant task of saying "no." Objections like these are automatic defense mechanisms that are easy excuses for not talking: "*I'm just about to walk into a meeting,*" or "*Someone just walked into my office.*"

The Legitimate Objection. The legitimate objection is one that the salesperson is powerless to overcome. Legitimate objections usually take the form of reasons why the prospect doesn't have the time to listen, the authority to buy, or a real need for the product. This is when you get the real objection, but it isn't necessarily the first objection you've heard. A sample of a legitimate objection could be: "*I made a purchase with a competitor and I'm set.*"

When Your Prospect Goes Radio Silent

You've had a great conversation with a prospect, and receive all the right buying and interest signals. Everything is clicking, connecting, and aligning with their needs and your solution. You capture the moment and progress to the next steps. They ask you to put a proposal together or tell you they are going to speak with a few more people or schedule a meeting—things are moving along! You are satisfied, you forecast the deal, it's a qualified opportunity, you feel good, your manager is happy.

And then . . . the following week you try calling them. You follow up with a quick e-mail. You try to get them live. No response. Nothing. Nada. You try again a few days later, you poke around to see if they are out of town, you leave another message and shoot a quick one-sentence e-mail. You get in super early and try to get them before they turn their office lights on. You call around to see if they are in their office. You call their cell phone. No response.

Now what? Do you give up? Let go? Apply more pressure? Get frantic? Become desperate? Take it personally? Start stalking them? That's what going "radio silent" is all about. It's about not knowing and wondering what happened. Salespeople never do well not knowing, because it's their job to know.

The truth is, your prospect thinks about your solution, service, or product about 1/300th of the time, while you think about it 24/7. There are a trillion other things for them to think about—and face it, you are just not at the top of the list for them. And there's no real reason why you should be. Get over it!

Once you really understand this—it's not you, really!—you can let go of some anxiety. You can also learn new ways to stay in front of your prospect while allowing the person some time to be distant. That doesn't mean letting go of the deal. Quite the opposite: it means you keep requalifying the deal, verifying the hierarchy, and creating a compelling event that helps build a timeframe around their response.

THE FIVE CATEGORIES OF OBJECTIONS

Even with all the changes in the sales field, one thing remains steady: objections haven't changed in thirty years. They still fall under five main categories:

1. Need
2. Relationship
3. Authority
4. Product/Service
5. Price

Whew! At least something stays constant. If you take some time to diagnose the top objections you receive, and determine what categories they fall into, you will get some valuable insight. After all, through their objections you are learning your clients' needs and wants, dislikes, and fears—in short, everything you need to know in order to get them to buy. Let's look at each of these categories more closely.

Need

Occasionally, a customer's need has decreased since the last time you spoke with them. Markets change, sometimes overnight.

The objection may also lie in the customer's *perception* of need (or lack thereof). We all know multiple initiatives are sitting on everyone's agenda, and the urgency and need for your solution may easily take a backseat.

Objections You May Hear
- "This is not a priority; we have other technology projects that we need to do first."
- "We don't see a need for this type of solution."
- "I am not interested."
- "We're not ready to do anything right now."
- "We are very happy with our current solution."

Rebounding Solutions
- Qualify your prospects to determine the potential for a need.
- Create a strong phone introduction that develops urgency.
- Determine if the prospect really understands what you are calling about.
- Call wide at different levels.

Relationship

People do business with people they like. Your customer may be resisting simply because something went wrong with your relationship. It may be a lack of trust, of confidence, or of comfort with your personality. Although customers are more open to change than ever before, they also want to strengthen existing relationships with current vendors and partner with them in new ways. It may be tougher to displace the competition now.

Objections You May Hear

- "We've made a large investment in our current solution."
- "We have already developed our short list and it's too late to look at another vendor."
- "The vendor we use provides the connectivity we need."
- "You are not an approved vendor."

Rebounding Solutions

- Establish trust and rapport.
- Learn how to sell against your competition.
- Determine if the prospect needs to be sold first or educated first.
- Call wide at different levels.

Authority

Your caller may not be the final decision maker or may be a No-Po. When you determine their decision-making status in your information gathering, you should also identify the lead decision maker. The decision maker's ability to buy may also be impaired by such things as high interest rates, lack of space, or fluctuations in the business.

Objections You May Hear

- "Just e-mail me your information. If someone is interested, we'll call you."
- "I am not in charge of networking, call my administrator."
- "Our corporate headquarters buys solutions for our networks."
- "I can't get the higher level to approve of this project."

Rebounding Solutions
- ➤ Understand the various authority levels and learn the chain of command to include more decision makers.
- ➤ Present your product and align it to their "hot buttons."
- ➤ Early in the sale, set expectations that you plan to align at the highest level.

Product/Service

Customers are knowledgeable and picky. They have less patience with anything that is too complicated yet they expect more functionality than ever before. The worst reason for a customer to resist your efforts is that your product is inferior or your company has a bad reputation. If indeed this is true, this is a difficult situation to overcome.

Objections You May Hear
- ➤ "Your service offerings are too complicated."
- ➤ "This is overkill for what we need. We have a very small network."
- ➤ "We've had a bad experience with your company before."

Rebounding Solutions
- ➤ Provide opportunities to educate on your product/service.
- ➤ Provide a cost-effective solution for easy entry.
- ➤ Ask precision questions.
- ➤ Neutralize their fears by providing added value for what you can deliver.

Price

Not everyone can afford to buy what they truly need. That is why it is so important to qualify your prospect. If you thoroughly gather information on their budget and price range, you will be able to tell the difference between an excuse not to buy and a real inability to buy. On the other hand, studies show that customers don't always buy based on price. As a matter of fact, very few customers tend to be price-driven if they understand the value your product or service can bring.

Objections You May Hear

> ➤ "No budget, IPT is too expensive—we would have to replace all our phones."
> ➤ "Your company is way too expensive and we're very small."
> ➤ "It's too expensive and includes more features than we need."
> ➤ "Our budgets are frozen; we cannot make any purchases or new investments.

Rebounding Solutions

> ➤ Qualify price versus ownership.
> ➤ Determine if this is really a strong prospect that has potential.
> ➤ Spend more time creating value and less time talking about budget.
> ➤ Call at the highest level and learn the purchasing criteria.

Rethinking Price

In studies conducted on why salespeople lose deals, the actual price of the product or service continues to rank as the lowest reason. As you learned in Chapter 6, "Linking," the higher you climb on the hierarchy chain, the less likely it is for price to be an issue. If you align yourself with people who are powerless to buy, price will always be the main objection—making you hear "no" from people who cannot say "yes"!

It's time to rethink price, don't you think? Any time you feel you are getting hung up on price, the following "re" techniques will prevent your prospects from getting stuck on price issues:

> ➤ *Rethink their values.* Everyone wants to feel like they matter. To your prospect, getting recognized and rewarded by his or her boss for negotiating the best price is important.
> ➤ *Revise their fears.* Most people are satisfied with something average and are afraid to take a chance on something they're not familiar with. When prospects' fears range from leaving their comfort zone, to spending more money than the boss wants, to getting fired, they're more likely to passively avoid what they don't like than to actively pursue what they do want.

> *Refresh their thinking.* Show that frontline manager a solution that'll bring the big picture back into focus. When people competing for resources and recognition are faced with their daily obligations, they lose sight of the bigger picture. Pitching how you can help the manager's company increase profitability is more meaningful when it directly impacts his or her year-end bonus.

> *Respect their sense of feeling appreciated.* Prospects feel overworked and underrespected. All they ask is that you make them look good. Provide them with solutions that'll take paperwork off their desks and keep their bosses happy with them, and they'll be happy with you.

> *Reinvent the customer's definition of the lowest TOTAL cost.* Instead of just showing the up-front, out-of-pocket cost for the company, show how the lowest *total* cost results from on-time delivery; faster time to market; support; quality; peace of mind with increased efficiency; ease of use; and reduced downtime, overhead, and labor.

> *Refocus questions to uncover what your customers value.* Understand what makes customers tick; see what's really driving them. In other words, ask more precision questions. You'll find out what they really want and why they want it, as opposed to what they're telling you they want.

THE E-MAIL OBJECTION

Most of the objections you receive will be delivered via e-mail—especially if you are using e-mail as a prospecting vehicle. These electronic rejections can be very short or quite detailed. Here are some examples of rejection e-mails you may receive throughout the sales cycle:

```
Hi Helen,
We decided to renew our annual contract with another
vendor, and although we liked your new features, we
cannot afford the downtime involved in a new imple-
mentation.

Thanks for your follow-up,
Alexandra
```

Hi Bob,

I believe we will be holding off for the moment.

Thank you for the proposal and we will consider it in the future if the need arises.

Jamie

Ryan,

Your web demo was great and the product seems more robust than what we actually need at this time.

We've decided to keep things as they are. I will be in touch with you if things change in the near future.

Lisa Lloyd

Hi Sue,

Due to our recent acquisition, we are not making any purchasing decisions through the end of the year.

Thanks for your follow-through,
Lindsay

Hi Julie,

Budgets are frozen through the end of year.

Carolyn

So: Do you send these e-mails directly to trash? Absolutely not! The minute you receive these types of e-mails, say, "This is an opportunity." You can actually earn more time from this e-mail and open up an opportunity for the future.

Pick Up the Phone

As soon as you get the e-mail, quickly make a call. You are still fresh in your prospect's mind—they just sent you the e-mail, so they're probably near a phone—and it's the perfect forum to start a dialogue. And remember—the people saying "no" are not always the ones who can say "yes."

Once you've engaged the prospect in conversation, keep these tips in mind:

- Create a safe conversation that encourages and anticipates potential objections.
- Listen and be sure to understand what the prospect's concerns are. Once you review the objection, listen to the entire objection.
- Ask for clarification from the prospect if you hear certain words and phrases that seem fuzzy. Ask lots of precision questions to make sure you get to the real objection. Clarify to understand the objection by rephrasing or paraphrasing it.
- Change, adapt, and revitalize your message to prevent common objections.
- Invite responses in a nondefensive manner. This helps open up to honest levels of communication. Gain confirmation and agreement from your prospect.
- Don't argue with or attack the customer. Empathize. Be respectful. Avoid getting defensive and overreacting. This is not personal.
- Try not to move into solutions mode too quickly.
- Keep asking more questions.

Cubicle Chronicles

─────────────────── Comeback Pack ───────────────────

The next time you're faced with an objection, grab a response out of this Comeback Pack. Better yet, study it *before* you get an objection so that you're prepared to counter effectively. These are what I've found to be the most common objections. The rebuttal questions are not just defensive statements; they are specifically designed to help you better understand exactly where the prospect stands so that you can use the objection as an opportunity to create rapport and keep moving through the sales cycle. Pick one rebuttal question from each category that best complements your style.

"I don't have time to talk."

> "No problem, I'll be brief. Can you tell me what you have in place in terms of [your product/service category]?"

> "Sure, I understand. So, before we schedule another time to talk, could you give me some information about your objectives and requirements?"

> "I appreciate your time constraints. Could I confirm that you are the right person to speak to about this? If not, could you share with me who might be?"

> "I understand things are hectic for you. When is the best time to get in touch with you, and what should I be prepared to discuss?"

> "I know that you're very busy. What is your recommendation to me for getting in touch with you?"

> "When would be a good time to talk about your objectives and requirements?"

> "If now's not a good time, when would be a more convenient time for you?"

> "Is there a better time? Great. What should I be ready to discuss with you?"

> "I have my calendar out. Can we set up a time to talk when you'll be available?"

> "Why don't we schedule a call at [time] on [day] so we can focus on your objectives?"

"I'm not interested."

> "Really? What have you heard about [name of your company]?"

> "What is your familiarity with [your company's] products? What do you think about these products?"

> "Let's say that [name of your company] had a product that fit your needs. What would be the process for consideration?"

- ➤ "I understand. Would you be the right person to speak with about [your product or service category] initiatives for your organization?"
- ➤ "I'm responding to your initial interest from our website. Could you please help me to understand what drove you to download some information?"
- ➤ "I'm just curious—what are your top objectives?"
- ➤ "How can I go about developing a relationship [or earning the right to] a long-term business relationship with you?"

"I don't have any needs at this time."

- ➤ "Let's say that you did have a need. What would be 'ideal' in terms of [name of your product category] solutions?"
- ➤ "What types of [name of your product category] projects are you currently working on?"
- ➤ "You must have a great current solution in place. What is it, and how is it working for you? What's one thing that could make it better?"
- ➤ "If you could have [name of competitor] do just one thing more—one enhancement—what would it be?"
- ➤ "When a need arises and you decide to implement changes, what is your company's process for researching new technologies?"
- ➤ "When is the next time you'll look into new technologies?"
- ➤ "When do you anticipate new projects or upgrades?"
- ➤ "What works best in establishing a business relationship with you?"

"We're just looking."

- ➤ "Great! What prompted your interest? Tell me about it."
- ➤ "What have you heard about our products?"
- ➤ "What have you heard about the tools and solutions we provide?"
- ➤ "What are you looking to accomplish?"

> "Could you tell me about your business?"

> "What types of projects are you currently working on?"

> "How can we go about earning the right to your business?"

> "Thanks for including us. What caused you to look?"

> "Can you tell me a little about your [name of your product category] initiatives today?"

> "We have the industry's widest range of [name of your product category] products. May I ask a few questions that might help us zoom in on your needs?"

"We are using [name of competitor]."

> "What do you like about [competitor]?"

> "Were you the person who chose your current solution? If not, who did? If so, when did you choose it and what were the key deciding factors? Did you look at [name of your company] solutions?"

> "Do you work with [competitor] throughout your company, or do you work with other vendors?"

> "If you could alter or improve what [competitor] is selling you, how would you?"

> "When do you evaluate what's new in the market to ensure that you're getting the best available solution?"

> "What would make you give [name of your company] the opportunity to do business with you?"

> "I'd like the opportunity to earn the right to some of your business. What are some of the things that would enhance your current situation?"

> "Would it be useful if I told you the top reason why other customers who were using our [competitor's] product decided to look into our solution?"

> "What changes, in your opinion, might occur in the future that could cause you to evaluate new options?"

> "How can I go about establishing a business relationship with you?"

"My boss doesn't want us to move forward on this."

- ➤ "What is your boss's familiarity with [name of your company]?"

- ➤ "I can understand your reluctance. What did you mention to your boss about [name of your company] and how well does he/she understand what we do?"

- ➤ "Please help me understand what is taking priority on this and why it isn't happening."

- ➤ "What have you recommended to your boss? Who is involved in the decision-making process? What decisions are they faced with? What is their familiarity with [name of your company]?" Can we schedule some time to meet with your boss and set up a conference call?"

"Your service offerings are too complicated."

- ➤ "Let's start over. What do you know so far about [name of your company]?"

- ➤ "Could you help me understand how you learn about and evaluate [name of your product category] solutions?"

- ➤ "What is your level of expertise with our solutions and products? I want to be a resource for you in understanding what we do."

- ➤ "I agree it can be overwhelming at first, and that's why I'm here to help. I can be a great resource for you. Why don't we walk through our offerings together?"

"Send me some information."

- ➤ "I'm happy to send you some literature. What are you looking for, and where will we go from there?"

- ➤ "Sure! What information shall I send? Why is that of interest to you? What will you be working on with regard to that? What's coming up with that particular product?"

- ➤ "I don't want to send information that isn't of use to you. What would be most helpful for me to send?"

- ➤ "Glad to. Mind if I ask a couple questions to zero in on your needs and what to send?"

- ➤ "I'd be happy to. What are you looking for?"
- ➤ "I'd like to send only information that you need. What should I send that would be of value to you? How do you educate yourself about these solutions?"
- ➤ "Sure. What is your current understanding of our products and services? What initiatives are you currently working on and what [name of your company] information would you like to receive?"
- ➤ "Great! Can we schedule a time next week to discuss the information I am about to send you?"

"You're too expensive."

- ➤ "Can you help me understand why you feel we are too expensive?"
- ➤ "What are you comparing us to? I want to be sure you are comparing apples to apples."
- ➤ "What are you basing that on?"
- ➤ "What have you looked at concerning 'price' versus 'cost'?"
- ➤ "Can you tell me about the research you've done and how you determined we are too expensive?"
- ➤ "Can you help me understand how you came to that conclusion?"
- ➤ "What needs to happen for you to feel more comfortable about a decision to use our products?"
- ➤ "Sounds like you are seriously comparing options. Why?"
- ➤ "Since I don't understand your application, I can't disagree. What type of solution are you leaning toward?"
- ➤ "I'm proud to be with this company, but I've learned that our products aren't for everyone. How did you come to that conclusion?"
- ➤ "If I could show you that we provide the greatest return on your investment, would the lowest price still win?"
- ➤ "You mentioned that the most important thing for you is price. How does that compare to what operations (or marketing, design, production, support) thinks is most important?"

- ➤ "What characteristics of this product are "must haves" for you and which are optional?"

"We don't have the budget."

- ➤ "How does your budget process work?"
- ➤ "If you did have the budget, which products would be of most interest to you?"
- ➤ "Does that mean that you don't have the money and couldn't get it under any circumstances, or do you need more justification to include us in your budget? How can I help you in that process?"
- ➤ "What have you looked at regarding 'price' versus 'cost'?"
- ➤ "What if you found that our products pay for themselves in a very short period of time?"
- ➤ "How can I help you justify the cost when you look at the benefits?"
- ➤ "What information do you need to help your management feel more comfortable?"
- ➤ "The changes we've discussed would result in an increase in profits. What would you do with that increase in available funding?"

"We had a bad experience with [name of your company] in the past."

- ➤ "I'm sorry to hear that. What happened?"
- ➤ "Who was involved and what products did this impact?"
- ➤ "Was there any resolution?"
- ➤ "What caused your disappointment and how did [name of your company] not exceed your expectations?"
- ➤ "What can I do to assure you this will not happen again and regain your trust?"
- ➤ "How can I best meet your expectations and regain your confidence?"
- ➤ "How can I go about establishing a business relationship with you?"

> "What would make you give [name of your company] the opportunity to do business with you?"

> "I'd like the opportunity to earn the right to some of your business. What are some of the things that would enhance your current situation?"

"We are going to hold off and use our home-grown solution."

> "I can understand your decision. What types of requests are you receiving for faster and more reliable [name of your product category]?"

> "Many of our customers who decide to work with their home-grown solution find their needs are compromised. Have you taken this into consideration?"

> "Great decision, if you want to keep everything status quo. May I recommend you consider our solution?"

> "Were you the person who chose your current solution?"

> "When do you evaluate what's new in the market to ensure you're getting the best-available solution?"

> "Would it be useful if I shared with you reasons why most customers come to us after using their home-grown solution?"

> "What changes, in your opinion, might be in the future that could cause you to evaluate new options?"

HANDLING OBJECTIONS STRATEGIES

1. It's time for you to dig deeper to understand the objections you receive—especially when you lose deals.

2. Expect to be hit with an objection tidal wave as more will come at you in various forms and few will be sugarcoated.

3. The telephone is a transparent tool. Be aware of the objections you may be creating with your phone presence throughout the sales cycle.

4. Your negative self-talk may be creating more damage than you thought. Save your career by building yourself up instead of tearing yourself down.

5. If you see warning signs that your sale may be in danger, pay attention! Then take a deep breath, regroup, and take whatever action is needed to change this pattern.

6. Objections may be delivered in many ways: some are silent and some are spoken. Be ready to listen to what the customer is *really* telling you, and respond effectively.

7. All the objections you will ever receive will come from five major categories: need, relationship, authority, product/service, and price. Once you identify these categories, and learn specific rebuttals, you will be more confident when you hear them.

8. Price can sound like the biggest objection, but it's not. Refresh and revise your thinking on this.

9. Expect to receive more and more e-mail rejections. That's good! You can pick up the phone immediately, while you are still fresh in the customer's mind, and lead them back to the sale.

10. Keep the Comeback Pack at hand every time you make a call. These questions can be your objection survival guide in tough times.

CHAPTER 9

CLOSING

The Complex Road to Gaining Commitment

You can get everything in life you want if you will just help
enough other people get what they want.

—Zig Ziglar

In this chapter, you'll get valuable insight into:

⊘ Why closing is much more complex than ever before

⊘ How the skills you learned in this book lead to solid closing skills

⊘ How important it Is to match your sales process with your prospect's buying process

⊘ Why listening with "happy ears" can be harmful to your sale

⊘ Why gaining self-confidence is a daily habit

You'll learn tools and tactics to help you:

⊘ Analyze your sales funnel: build a high-quality, smoothly running funnel every month

⊘ Ask the most appropriate questions at each stage of the sales process, and especially when you hear closing signals

⊘ Create momentum via compelling events throughout the sales cycle

⊘ Get a daily dose of self-confidence

⊘ Get motivated, using end-of-quarter success stories of actual sales reps

Manager: "Gina, I need your numbers by noon today. We need to sit down and review what you have in for the month. What is your commit number?"

Gina: "Sure. I'm just waiting on a few deals to come through."

Manager: "How much has your forecast changed since last week?"

Gina: "There's been a bit of a fall-out due to the holidays."

Manager: "I can't afford any surprises at this stage. Can I help you close some of these deals? I'm counting on your numbers."

Gina: "I got a few small deals in, and I'm still waiting on BTB to come in. They said they would get something to me this month."

Manager: "Hi Marc, how are things looking? We're down to the wire this month and I could use some good news."

Marc: "I'm flying this month! Things couldn't be sweeter."

Manager: "Awesome! Tell me about those two deals with GGI Manufacturing and DTD Associates. Are you bringing them in this month?"

Marc: "Well, GGI is still waiting for us to help them with their on-site project and the DTD order is being reviewed by their legal team."

Manager: "When will we get the PO for that?"

Marc: "I left them a message and called my buyer, but he's been on vacation, so I'm hoping to hear back today."

Manager: "Hi, Sylvia. Are we still meeting later this afternoon to review your numbers?"

Sylvia: "Did you get a chance to review my e-mail request about SST Systems? I can build in consulting services if we can drop the price by 15 percent, because they want us to honor last year's price. Can you give me the green light on that?"

Manager: "Is that all that deal is riding on? Will you be able to bring it in this week if I approve the discount?"

Sylvia: "Definitely. Remember? I lost the other deal because we couldn't meet them on price, so before I e-mailed you on SST Systems, I asked them to give me a verbal and they did."

CLOSING MEANS MASTERING THE SALES PROCESS

No sales rep has actually told their manager, "The dog ate my homework," but when it comes time to review the pipeline and forecast, desperate excuses for not closing come pretty close.

Each week, your manager asks you the same questions: *"What's happening with that deal?" "When will you bring this in?" "Who have you been talking with?" "What's holding them back?" "If you give your client a 15 percent discount, do you think you can bring it in this month?"*

And each week, these managers hear the same answers from their reps: *"I'm just waiting on the purchase order . . ." "We are their vendor of choice . . ." "I'll bring this one in this afternoon. I just left them a message this morning . . ." "They're waiting until the end of the month for their discount."*

The pressure to close has never been greater, yet fewer inside reps are hitting quota. What's the disconnect?

Closing is where the rubber meets the road. If your sales process, and your prospect's buying process, have not been on target all the way, the deal won't close. Your ability to close a deal isn't about that last moment when the customer says "yes." It's about:

> Mastering your sales skills: the ones you've learned in this book
> Building and managing a healthy sales funnel that doesn't have you resorting to desperate discounting measures at the end of the month just to keep your job or make your manager happy
> Mastering your sales process: using your skills to shape deals through the various sales stages
> Understanding your customer

And, of course, it's about you: believing you really deserve the business, and your determination and belief that you will *not* lose the sale to your competitor or a "no decision"!

SALES 2.0: THE COMPLEX CLOSE

The crowded and noisy Sales 2.0 landscape does not make for a smooth road to closing. Reps are all vying with one another to get time with customers who routinely shut them down by opting out of meetings and deleting their carefully crafted e-mails or voice mails. Many reps that do get a few minutes to qualify don't dig deep enough to learn anything, or call wider to reconfirm. Or they cave to the objection du jour and move on. If they manage to make their way to center stage to present, they find they have a captive audience full of No-Po's. Add to that pushy and reactive managers who force their reps to beg for the business and you have the makings of the complex close.

Closing in Sales 2.0 requires accuracy, accountability, and efficiency. You need to know how to build a healthy pipeline and then keep your eye on the deal as it travels through sales stages that neatly align with your prospect's buying cycle. Gone are the days of the "puppy dog close," where you could charm your way to a close, or the "rolling pen close," where you could manipulate your buyer to sign on the dotted line. It's about listening with "honest ears" instead of "happy ears," and creatively justifying the cost of your solution. You can use the best of what Sales 2.0 has to offer—technology, process improvement, and sales knowledge—to do something deceptively simple: align the steps in the sales cycle with those in the buying cycle. This does a wonderful thing: it convinces the prospect that they are in control, which will encourage them to run *toward* your deal, not away from it.

MASTER YOUR SALES SKILLS

Remember all those skills you learned in the previous chapters? Some probably seemed basic, others were good refreshers, and a few may have been new to you. But as we said in the beginning of this book, each skill builds on the one that came before. And they've all been leading to one place: closing the deal. If you decided to bypass a skill along the way, this is when it will come back to bite you! Let's take one more ride through all these skills and review their impact when it comes to closing.

Time Management

The choices you make about your time are critical to your entire process. If you spend your time distracted, worrying, paralyzed, panicked, and calling without a plan, and then let reactive managers soak up your time nagging you about bringing business in, you'll never hit your numbers. This is like withdrawing money from your bank account again and again without making deposits. Pretty soon, you'll have nothing to draw on.

Be proactive! Start your month by building a well-thought-out territory plan that includes a list of target accounts and new opportunities. Then you can spend the rest of that month slowly chiseling away at it. Your strong momentum will help you build a solid pipeline that includes a good mix of small, medium, and large opportunities—all at different stages in the sales cycle. You'll find the closing process to be a lot calmer, more predictable, and much more accurate—every month.

Introducing

The "multiple-touch" rule we discussed in Chapter 2, in regard to introducing, is also the beginning of your path to closing—and it's a tool you'll use all along the way. If you are always thinking of something new to provide your prospect, then you won't pressure them so much when it comes time to close. You learned how to "show up" in this skill and realized this "opt-out" crowd can easily shut you out if you don't take the time to understand their business, their needs, their pressures. Keep doing this at the close! Do your homework. Stay fresh, positive, and upbeat with your messaging, and certainly remember to thank them when you bring the deal in.

Whether you call on the phone or send a quick e-mail, use power and results language to express your appreciation for their business. Thank and acknowledge them with words or phrases such as *perfect timing, great choice, thanks for your business, we're excited to get started,* and *the start of a mutually rewarding partnership* to validate their decision to buy.

Navigation

There's no doubt that No-Po's will severely clog up your sales funnel. The faster you can sniff them out, the quicker you can say your good-byes, leave the No-Po zone, and enter the clean funnel zone instead.

Build your 2x2 org chart and write out an entire list of key contacts for the organization early in the sales process, but keep reviewing it and stay flexible. If you realize belatedly that you stuck with a No-Po too long, review your list of original contacts. You probably had the power buyer's name the whole time. Power moves and hides. Keep searching, and don't be afraid to switch horses no matter where you are in the stream.

Questioning

Questioning—approaching the qualification process from the inside out—is the heart of the sales funnel. Instead of chasing anything that looks like an opportunity, begging for discounts, or adding more leads to the pipeline, work smart: establish an efficient lead qualification process that is based on quality versus quantity. By quickly qualifying and converting opportunities, you will reduce the length of the sales cycle and increase the relationship and trust that fuels the sale. And remember that the answers to your qualification criteria will later be your doorways to closing.

Listening

The damage that "happy ears" will cause on your pipeline is big. If all you hear is what you want to hear, you will never understand why you keep losing sales. If you keep selling, selling, selling, jumping in when the customer is trying to tell you something, and figuring that if you just keep talking they will buy your product, you will lose sales.

Listen to what customers are really telling you—and they will tell you everything you need to know. You can work with this information and ride it straight to closing. Listen for the prospect's pain, understand its implications, document it, and work with it to create compelling events.

Linking

You finally found the power buyer. But just because they let you in and listened to your story, don't stop there. Create a solid relationship with them throughout the sales process. Stay on their radar by providing them with value all along the way. Adjust your messaging to their language to put yourself on an equal footing and hold their attention until the end.

Presenting

Presenting is where you make the case for everything you've been telling prospects all along. If you bore them with endless PowerPoint slides, or lose them through a disorganized meeting, they will not be returning your calls. A smart, informative presentation will give them a better understanding of your company and product, and why it is perfect for them. In fact, it will clinch the deal. Plan, plan, plan, and then follow through.

Handling Objections

You will always get slammed by objections. Don't let them demoralize you halfway to the sale! If you do, you will never get to closing.

The trick is to learn to distinguish which are valid and which are self-inflicted. Objections do not have to be showstoppers. Know your comebacks, learn them, and use them to show prospects why their objections are ungrounded, or how your product or service can meet their needs in ways they never considered.

Partnering

We'll talk about partnering in the final chapter of this book. Although partnering is strictly a part of your sales process, in many organizations inside salespeople are regularly paired up with field partners. If you and your field partner are at each other's throats, as happens far too often, closing a sale may remain just always out of reach. In a nutshell, you have the choice to either get along with your field partner or not. It is possible to create a relationship where the two of you make magic together, complementing each other's qualities, and we'll look at how this is possible in the final chapter.

BUILD A HEALTHY SALES FUNNEL

Every salesperson has heard of the sales funnel. Opportunities start at the top of the funnel, and as they get qualified they move down the funnel. Conversion rates vary depending on how long the sales cycle is, how large the average deal size is, how many decision makers are involved in the purchasing process—and how skillful you are at managing the sales process.

How the Funnel Works

A sales funnel is shaped like an upside-down cone: wide at the top and narrow at the bottom, which tells you right away that, out of a wide field, only a few sales will get through. New "suspect" opportunities come in at the top. They travel down by getting qualified, become converted into "prospects," and eventually close at the bottom of the funnel.

The funnel houses every opportunity you are currently working, all at different stages of the qualification process. As they advance through the sales stages, these suspects turn into prospects and eventually become forecasted to close. Your goal is to create pipeline momentum with a variety of opportunities and manage them through the funnel until they close. Simple?

Not every opportunity you put into the funnel converts to a closed deal. Because everyone you talk to isn't a hot prospect, you must qualify your "suspects" to eventually become prospects. The percentage of sales opportunities that actually end up closed is called your "closing ratio." A 25 percent closing ratio means that you close one out of every four sales you start.

Your ability to build and manage a smart funnel is the key to closing. Putting to work the skills you learned in the previous chapters will help you grow your sales, advance them through the sales stages, and bring them to closure.

Sales Funnel 101

What's in your funnel is important. But what matters is what is moving and changing in your funnel—because a funnel that's really working for you never sits still.

Funnels can look very different depending on the time of the month. Watch that you do not fall into some bad funnel habits. The funnels in Figure 9-1 all have something wrong with them. What is it?

Developing your funnel is important to your long-term survival in sales. So what's the perfect funnel? As pictured in Figure 9-2, a healthy funnel has a good mix of suspects and prospects at different levels. You're looking for quality, not necessarily quantity. If you want to achieve a healthy funnel, you must dedicate a few hours each week to building your funnel, and dedicate hours every day to growing it. Be careful not to clog your funnel with dirty data, or let leads incubate too long without properly qualifying them.

Good Funnel Habits Add Momentum to Your Pipeline

Your sales funnel will take care of you if you take care of it. Keep reviewing your funnel throughout the month, continually asking: What's in it? Are the deals big, small, or a healthy mix? What is the value of each deal?

These good funnel management habits are critical because—as we discussed way back in Chapter 1, "Time Management"—when bad habits settle in, the momentum slows, and you create a funnel that is empty or clogged.

Figure 9-1. Sales Funnel Analysis

	Funnel 1: Very little activity. This funnel has a lot of unqualified leads or "suspects" floating on the top that haven't been qualified. This may be early in the sales cycle, or the funnel may belong to a new rep, or it may be that leads were simply dumped into the bucket. Clearly, it illustrates very little activity has taken place and nothing is ready to close.
	Funnel 2: Deals floating around. This funnel has more activity: there's a combination of "suspects," and "prospects" are mostly small deals floating at different stages of the sales cycle. Still, nothing is moving down to the close. This funnel may belong to a rep that is busy but lacks the focus to take something, grow it, and close it.
	Funnel 3: One deal is clogging the funnel. This funnel has very few deals—mostly suspects, and one very large prospect, which is the deal that is in the process of closing. The rep has been extremely focused on closing that big deal and has let other business slide. Once that big deal has closed, they will have to pick up their momentum to rebuild their funnel.
	Funnel 4: One big deal is not enough. This is the most dangerous and risky funnel. The rep is solely focused on that one big deal, investing too much of their time on it and ignoring everything else in the process—in fact, everything else has disappeared. Picking up momentum in this situation will be very difficult.
	Funnel 5: Small deals, little skill. This funnel shows more movement but nothing is closing. Most of these are suspects. The ones that are closing could be "low-hanging fruit," which means they are closing without much effort from the salesperson and may have just closed on their own. This funnel doesn't demonstrate the qualification skills that show the deal growing and moving down the funnel until it closes.

Figure 9-2. A Healthy Sales Funnel

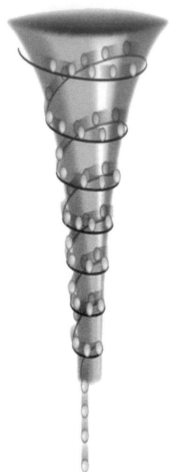

Poor funnel-building skills look like this:

Week 1: Take a rest from the end-of-month closing frenzy because the adrenaline has been pumping for days just getting orders in.

Week 2: Review your pipeline and start building it, since you've been so focused on closing and not focused on building.

Week 3: Go to meetings and trainings, and work on reports. You need to formally communicate and set new priorities and objectives and get the teams geared up for another big push.

Week 4: Panic sets in and you start selling. It's back to the end of the month and the cycle continues.

The scenario above illustrates an all-too-common occurrence: a funnel built by a reactive salesperson whose bad habits result in lost momentum and a lot of wheel-spinning.

A better way? Be proactive. Use your time management chops to schedule your funnel-building activities as a regular part of every week.

Good funnel-building skills look like this:

Week 1: Continue to ride the great adrenaline wave. Make introductory calls, learn new tools, expand your reach through social networking, and schedule some appointments, demos, and presentations with busy decision-makers who need a two-to-three-week lead time.

Week 2: Begin an aggressive call campaign to new and existing customers to create urgency early. Your primary focus will be on generating quotes and following up.

Week 3: Prioritize! Your clear goals and selling priorities will help you make strong choices to not attend all meetings and trainings.

Week 4: Approach this week with more confidence, knowing you're ahead of the rest. Since you've made your number, you get to help the team and your region with more accelerators.

Once you get a handle on your momentum, it's time to convert your suspects into qualified prospects and start building your sales forecast.

Funnel Math

Sales 2.0 realities mean that today's funnels must be two to three times larger than they used to be because there is more fallout. If you know your closing ratio, you can get an idea of the size of your prospecting pipeline. For example:

If your annual sales target or quota is $1 million

And your average sale is $20K:

You'll need fifty sales to make your quota.

If your closing ratio is 25 percent:

You'll need four hot prospects for every sale.

You'll need two hundred potential opportunities in the top of your sales funnel.

MASTER YOUR SALES PROCESS: THE KEY TO ACCURATE FORECASTING

Having a formal sales process is the single biggest contributor to sales success. An effective sales process helps you track your opportunities, create a common language between you and your sales manager, and make accurate forecasts. The better you can define where your deals are in the sales process, the stronger awareness you will have of activities that drive results, with less possibilities for surprises along the way, and the more confidence your manager will have in your forecast. In fact, you will reach a higher percentage in your forecast because you can direct all your energies to the right activities. You will penetrate more opportunities because you will have a better understanding of the customers' business and where they are heading.

CSO Insights' 2008 "Sales Performance Optimization" report found that firms without a formal sales methodology showed a lower conversion rate, resulting in fewer closes on sales. The firms that had a formal process in place outperformed the rest in terms of accurately targeting prospects, properly qualifying leads, effectively presenting features and benefits, effectively cross-selling and up-selling, selling value and avoiding excessive discounting, and effectively introducing new products. In addition, the report indicated that process-centric sales teams outperform sales teams that depend entirely upon the talent of their sales executives.

THE SIX STAGES OF A SALES PROCESS

Different companies have different names and definitions for their sales stages. Most are aligned with their automation tool, such as Salesforce.com (SFDC). Depending on the size and complexity of the deal, a sales process can have between three and eight sales stages. But it doesn't matter how many there are or what they're called as long as everyone agrees and understands each stage.

I generally see six distinct stages:

1. Identify
2. Discover
3. Validate
4. Solve
5. Present
6. Close

The questions included after the description of each one, below, will help you determine what stage in the sales cycle your deal is in, and how it is doing. Work with the qualification criteria from Chapter 4, "Questioning" (pages 91–96), and be sure you have formed strong bonds of understanding with your various committee members.

Stage 1: Identify (10 Percent Toward Closing). The first stage in the sales cycle involves preliminary qualification and profiling of the prospect's business issues. This is your first opportunity to place your business squarely in front of potential customers, since they'll likely search for both your company as well as your industry online.

Before you leave this stage, you should have solid answers to the following:

- Who is the customer?
- What is their organization and industry?
- Who are the stakeholders?
- Have you contacted them?
- What are the customer's plans and pain points?
- What opportunities have you identified?
- What are the next steps?
- Has the customer agreed to the next steps?

Stage 2: Discover (25 Percent Toward Closing). During this second stage in the sales cycle, you and the prospect are in clear agreement on their business needs and technical requirements. The prospect confirms the value of the potential solution.

Before you leave this stage, you should have solid answers to the following:

- What is their current technical environment?
- What type of solutions do they have in place?
- What primary applications are they currently using?
- Who is the project champion or executive sponsor?
- Who is the power buyer?
- Have you identified other contacts on the decision-making committee and asked what their role is?
- Has the project champion admitted the need for your solution?
- Did the sponsor agree to evaluate your solution?
- Do you have some idea of the project timeline?

Stage 3: Validate (50 Percent Toward Closing). The third stage in the sales cycle brings you to the halfway point. In this stage, you present a compelling, crisp, differentiated concept with a credible and quantifiable return on investment. You have a detailed understanding of the prospect's approval process, and they have agreed to partner on your solution.

Before you leave this stage, you should have solid answers to the following:

- How well do they understand your product/service and solution?
- Have the technical issues been discussed?
- Has the power buyer admitted to the business gap and outlined specific needs?
- What other solutions has the prospect researched, considered, or implemented?
- Has the competition been identified? What other options is the prospect considering?

- Have you proposed the appropriate solution and linked it to the customer's needs?
- Have you identified the prospect's pain points and determined how your solution will help?
- What is the compelling event, need, or issue that is driving their interest?
- What are the current problems motivating them to look at this solution?
- Can the power buyer articulate the vision of the solution?
- Have you validated your understanding of the business needs with the power buyer?
- Has the power buyer shared his or her budget plan with you?
- Has the power buyer stated support of your concept as a possible solution?
- Did the power buyer share his or her approval process and selection criteria? What is it?
- Has the purchasing process been identified? Do you have knowledge of where the funds will come from?
- Has the power sponsor validated the ROI? Will they have final sign-off?
- Has the action plan been agreed to with the power buyer?
- Has the timeframe been discussed?
- Have you confirmed how this type of project gets final approval and what would be the next step to move it forward to the decision makers?
- Have you asked who will release the funds for the purchase?
- Has the budget cycle been identified?
- Have pricing issues been analyzed and determined to be acceptable to the customer?
- Can you identify any deal stoppers? If so, what are they?

Stage 4: Solve (75 Percent Toward Closing). In this stage, you develop a detailed technical solution that supports the compelling, crisp, differentiated concept you developed in Stage 3.

Before you leave this stage, you should have solid answers to the following:

- Has the customer selected your service/product?
- Has the customer communicated a possible intent to purchase?
- Has the customer validated the approach and unique selling proposition?
- Have you included the value justification?
- Have you asked for a verbal agreement for the business?
- Has the final proposal been issued?
- Is the committee leaning toward a final product decision very soon?
- Has the funding been secured and approved?
- Does your power buyer have the authority to buy?

Stage 5: Present (90 Percent Toward Closing). During this next-to-last stage in the sales cycle, you will present the offer tied to the prospect's requirements to the decision makers. Your goal is to effectively handle any business and technical objections to gain prospect acceptance.

Before you leave this stage, the following must happen:

- The power customer agrees that your recommendation has met their requirements and that they see unique value of your solution.
- You answer all business and technical objections to the customer's satisfaction.
- You receive a verbal commitment.
- Contract negotiations are moving forward.
- You have done everything to ensure this step is completed.

Stage 6: Close (100 Percent Complete!). In this final stage of the sales cycle, the prospect has agreed to the terms and conditions of the sale and has signed the contract. The opportunity is technically closed and booked in the system. But you still have some questions to answer to make sure all is well.

Before you leave this stage, you must have solid answers to the following:

- ⊘ Has an order been received and booked into the system?
- ⊘ Have all contractual terms and conditions been agreed to?
- ⊘ Is there a signed contract?
- ⊘ Are the appropriate approval signatures in place?
- ⊘ Has the partner issued a PO to your organization?
- ⊘ Have you done everything to ensure this step is completed?

UNDERSTAND YOUR CUSTOMER'S BUYING AGENDA

You've learned your sales skills, reviewed your funnel, and located your deal in the sales process. What's left? The customer!

Align Your Sales Process with the Prospect's Buying Process

Understanding your prospect's decision-making process—who's involved, who the key stakeholders are, and who makes the final call—is critical to your sales success. Best-practice companies manage their selling activities from a solid understanding of how their customers buy: not only buying patterns and habits, but also details related to the steps customers take in making the purchase decision.

According to SiriusDecisions' "Sales 2.0: Don't Believe the Hype" research brief, "Buyers, not salespeople, now control the flow of information, making them savvier than ever before. They have developed their own processes for assessing, selecting, and negotiating with vendors, and added a number of formal and informal decision makers to this multi-month or multi-quarter process, challenging traditional sales cycle and sale methodology thinking to embrace this new paradigm."

The customer's buying process actually maps well to the six stages of the selling process we just reviewed:

1. Recognize business strategy
2. Define requirements

3. Evaluate alternatives
4. Select solution
5. Negotiate
6. Implement solution

Understanding where your customer is in their process will help you align solidly with their needs. Take the time to do it.

Drop the Happy Ears and Listen to the Truth

I bet this sounds familiar: Your deal slips into the next month because it was a few weeks' shy of closing. You are sure it's going to happen, but get disappointed on the last day of the month. Then you have to face your manager and explain why you missed your number. No matter what your excuse, the real reason is happy ears!

Listening to what you want to believe instead of what the customer is really saying is one of the biggest causes of inaccurate forecasting. We've talked about it in regard to navigating and listening, and it bears repeating here. When your prospect says, *"We like it and want to bring it in"* or *"I'll get that Purchase Order signed by next week,"* you bank on that as their final answer—only to be disappointed when the deal doesn't close.

The questions I've listed in every single stage of the sales process are designed to get you to stop listening with happy ears and nail down the truth.

Closing Signal Questions

The closing stage is the riskiest stage of the sales process. It's risky for the buyers, but they rarely want to admit it. Instead, they lie to you about their intentions. Many salespeople believe the deal is going to happen just because they get a verbal commitment—but this is not the time to coast. Drill down with more questions and get specific. These closing signal questions are specifically designed to help you better understand exactly where the prospect stands so that you can use their response to make an accurate forecast.

"We are ready to buy."
"I'm happy to hear that. Do you mean you are ready to buy this month? What takes place from research to implementation?

"I'm submitting this to purchasing."
"Great news! Please tell me more about your purchasing process: who is involved, who signs off, how many people are in the committee, will any of the committee members be on vacation, what might get in the way?

"It's just a matter of the paperwork."
"Please walk me through your procurement process: who gets involved, what other departments must review the paperwork, legal, finance, and so on?"

"I'm going to recommend we make this purchasing decision."
"Thanks. Who will you recommend this to? What reaction do you anticipate? How many will you discuss this with and what communication vehicle will be utilized? Formal presentation, phone meeting, e-mail?"

"I want to get moving on this."
"Perfect timing! I want to make it happen as well"

Look for the Compelling Event

A deal rarely closes unless there is a compelling event: something that is driving the opportunity to close. It may be something external (the customer is opening four new offices) or monetary (your contact will get his bonus by the end of the year if he negotiates this discount with a vendor).

When you dig for pain, it is critical that you ask questions such as, *"What happens if your timeframes are not met?"* or *"What is driving you to make this decision at this time, and what happens if you don't?"*

When you can pinpoint the compelling event, you can use it to drive the sale to closing. If there really is no compelling event, it may be a harder sell.

Move Away from Price and Talk Value

When budgets are tight, expectations are high and risk-taking is low. Buyers want to know the core value of their investment in your solution. You must talk ROI.

Explain how your solution starts paying for itself the minute they commit. Tell them what they can expect to receive after one week, one month, one year. Discuss a specific product, project, or process of theirs, and explain how your organization contributes to their profit picture or saves them money. Example: *"Within thirty days of implementation, you will experience immediate returns, with less hours of downtime and an increased sense of confidence."*

Remember That Customers Are Not Always Driven By Price

We've trained our customers to wait until the end of the month or end of the quarter to get their discount, and this is a hard cycle to break—especially if they are No-Po's who will string you along and request more discounts because they ultimately must sell it to their boss.

Yet more and more research indicates customers are not always driven by price when they purchase something. According to CSO Insights' 2008 "Inside Sales Performance Optimization" report, the majority of the five hundred firms that participated in the study claimed that their reps continue to struggle with discounting to get the sale. They say that buyers have come to the table better informed, more demanding, and facing more scrutiny on every purchase. Add to that more competition and pressure to close as many deals as possible, and reps are often quick to reach for the desperate discount lever.

But discounting doesn't solve anything. This is the time to get creative and negotiate nonmonetary incentives. Before you give up and chase the discount, ask yourself these questions:

- ➤ Is there value in my product or service for my prospect?
- ➤ What is the hard dollar value (ROI)?
- ➤ What other value is there (prestige, safety)?

> ➤ Does the prospect understand and value the benefits of my product or service?

> ➤ Is a decision to buy my offering better than a decision to create my offering in-house?

> ➤ What risk to the prospect must I minimize or alleviate in regard to this buying decision (financial, time of implementation, opportunity cost, prestige, and so on)?

> ➤ What urgency have I created to encourage the prospect to move forward now (time to market, discounts, delivery, incentives, guarantees, and so on)?

> ➤ Why is buying my product or service a better decision than moving forward with my competitor or taking no action at all?

WORK OUT YOUR SELF-CONFIDENCE MUSCLES

The selling landscape is brutal. When you work in a sales organization that only considers you as good as your last sale, it can be grueling. No wonder it stabs at your insecurities, your self-esteem, and your confidence. You are not alone! Every salesperson struggles with confidence at some time during his or her sales career.

I like to approach building confidence like a workout: strengthen your ego, sculpt your resilience, and energize your drive. Here are my ten workout tips for increasing self-confidence:

1. *Get some "yes" going.* I like to start by conditioning myself to hear "yes," so that I will eventually come to expect it. I therefore initiate things that it will be easy to get others to say "yes" to—like inviting good friends to dinner, organizing a camping trip, or volunteering my time.

2. *Visualize winning.* Visualization is powerful. I like to visualize what I want to work toward. I may cut out a picture of a new car and tack it to the wall where I can see it every morning, visualize my name at the top of the sales whiteboard, visualize accepting an award from the President's Club, or visualize myself presenting confidently at a meeting.

3. *Dress up.* I am still amazed at how many inside sales reps dress so casually while their field counterparts dress more formally. Just because your prospects can't see you doesn't mean you need to be so casual. What you choose to wear has a direct impact on how you feel about yourself, which in turn will affect your performance. Dress sharp to sell smart!

4. *Use the power of knowledge.* The more you know, the more confidence you have when conversing with your prospects. When you take the opportunity to learn, you naturally develop more confidence. Do your homework about the person or organization you are calling before you make the call. They will always be impressed, and you will feel good about yourself.

5. *Bounce back.* To be resilient means to be both strong and flexible. Bouncing back from rejection helps you move on. Rejection is part of the job. Don't take it personally! Understand it, learn from it, and bounce back.

6. *Focus on what is ahead.* Negativity can easily deflate you and can keep you down. Instead, focus on what is ahead and the possibilities that lie in front of you. Set small goals and make them happen. The larger goals will follow.

7. *Find a positive, supportive mentor.* Surrounding yourself with negativity will always drag you down. I like to align myself with positive people, and I've been lucky in my life to have invaluable mentors who have provided inspiration, direction, and support. Good mentors are committed to your success and they can champion your efforts. Your mentor can be your sounding board, supporter, listener, adviser, teacher, and friend.

8. *Ask for happy customer testimonials.* There's no better way to strengthen your belief in your product, solution, or company than to call your existing customers and ask what they like most. It will not only help build your story about your service, it will help build your confidence in yourself as an effective salesperson. If you did it before, you can do it again!

9. *Did I really say that?* The next time you describe a personal experience, listen to the words you choose and how you position your story. Is your tone or intention confident? Do you boast about yourself, exag-

gerate to gain acceptance, or put yourself down and complain? You'll see how people are reacting to your confidence or lack of it by their response. Pay attention, and learn to speak positively about yourself and your product.

10. *Be a sales hero.* Everyone has a story about the moment they became a sales hero—one event that attracted them to sales as a career. Here's mine: When I was about twenty-five and had no desire to ever be in sales, my boss announced at the last minute that he could not be at the upcoming trade show and that I would be on my own. I had spent months inviting people to this show, but never thought I would be selling—I was just doing the "behind-the-scenes work." That trade show turned out to be the highest-grossing revenue-producing show we did in years. I was hooked. Stories like these, and memories of a time when you were successful build confidence and bring inspiration.

<hr />——————— **End-of-Quarter Motivational Success Stories**———————<hr />

It's end of quarter, and we interviewed several star inside sales warriors who agreed to share their secrets for exceeding quota.

Marvelous Marilyn is in full momentum: Marilyn believes that making every day and every month count as though it were quarter end is her secret. She starts her quarter building a strategic plan of attack and just reaps the benefits the rest of the time. She has trained her buyers not to wait until the last minute, because she rarely discounts. But she negotiates good creative terms with them and brings the deals in—every time. She stays organized and establishes a strong momentum.

Discounting isn't an option for Dave: Dave's secret is to never hang out with No-Po's, so he never fights price battles. He sells on value and sells high up on the food chain. His customers never ask for discounts and he never offers. Instead, he is very well positioned with the power buyers and has built trust in his relationships that will last a lifetime with them. They give him straight answers, and he is always assured his deals are solid and they come in as forecasted.

It's a cakewalk for consistent Carla: You can always count on Carla's steady numbers each month. She is the most accurate, organized, and consistent player on the team. Because Carla keeps her eyes on the prize and manages each deal through the entire process, she may not have a huge funnel of opportunities, but the ones she is working on are high quality, tight, clean, and solid. Carla is confident, so closing is a non-event for her—she is already doing it all right every step of the way.

CLOSING STRATEGIES

1. Closing is not some mysterious event. If you stay on top of your deals all the way through the sales process, the close will happen.
2. Stay focused on the skills you've learned in this book. They have each been designed to lead you to the close. Just follow them, and you will keep your eye on the prize.
3. Build a healthy sales funnel that includes a solid assortment of small- , medium- , and large-sized opportunities.
4. Be ambitious. Build a large sales funnel to allow for potential fallout and strive to exceed your numbers.
5. Follow your sales process. Understand what to expect at each stage so you will never be surprised.
6. Align with your prospect's buying cycle. Position yourself well with decision makers and other influencers to ensure your deal is solid.
7. Listen to your prospect's pain, remember it, and use it to create compelling events. Drop the "happy ears"—they will get you in trouble.
8. Stay focused on the compelling event. Once you have this identified, use it to help your prospects realize the importance of having your solution in place by a certain time.

9. Stay confident. Do what you can every day to keep building your self-esteem and faith in your ability to close deals. A good, positive attitude will relieve stress.

10. Closing is all about momentum: stay organized, focused, and persistent.

CHAPTER 10

PARTNERING
Conscious Collaboration

If we are together nothing is impossible.
If we are divided all will fail.

—Winston Churchill

In this chapter, you'll get valuable insight into:

- The reasons some partnerships are set up to fail
- The attributes you bring to a healthy partnership
- How agreements and expectations with your field partner build your value
- How social networking and strategic alliances can increase your sales viability

You'll learn tools and tactics to help you:

- Articulate the value of a team selling approach
- Identify strong and weak partnerships
- Determine your partner-readiness criteria
- Design agreements for strong partnering
- Be alert and creative when looking to form a strategic alliance
- Commit to being responsible as you grow your social networks

"I can't believe he never followed through on the deal I sent him weeks ago. The customer wanted to meet with someone and my rep never followed up to schedule something."

"Why can't she just read the notes in the database? I diligently inputted the entire profile by including the tasks and activities and she never even bothered to read through it all."

"I called my field rep to introduce myself to our territory and he said I was the fourth new inside rep he had in two years and he is tired of sharing. He suggested I work on my own list and he work on his."

"I told my field partner about the deal and she ran off with it and wants all the credit. Then she had the nerve to tell my manager that she never gets any leads from me."

"My field partner always calls frantically on his way to his appointment and wants me to explain the history of the account and prep him over the phone. His urgency is not my urgency."

"I can't believe I've been assigned to the Northeast territory and the rep I have to support is Joe Nardo! That guy is impossible to work with. No one can stand him."

. . . .

This just in: The inside salesperson is no longer held captive by their assigned territory and field partners! Gone are the days when you sat impatiently waiting to hear back from your field partner on whether you could contact their customer. Gone are the days when your worth was measured by the quantity of leads you delivered. Today, inside sales *owns* the partnerships, and the partnerships have no boundaries.

That's right. Now is your time to partner proactively—making the contacts, building a healthy sales funnel, presenting like a pro, and blazing the path to deals that close. Effective partnering today is not just about getting along with your field partner, following their lead, waiting to be told what to do next, or entering their orders into the system. Your new role is to collaborate as an equal with field sales, to expand your footprint in the organization by creating strategic alliances that help *you* make sales, and, of course, to stay current and visible by expanding your social networks. The bottom line is that *you can shape your partnership's success or failure.* That's what the partnering skill is all about.

In this chapter, we explore partnering with the field, strategic partnerships, and social networking partnerships. We also explore your role within the traditional inside and field sales structure, and see how earning your stripes at partnering teaches you the importance of collaborating for the common good of the territory, the team, the organization, the customer, and yourself.

SALES 2.0: TECHNOLOGY ENABLES COLLABORATION

The Sales 2.0 environment makes possible a new level of collaboration. Although the organization's inside and field reps may be scattered geographically, the tools they share bring them together, making a new level of partnering possible.

A recent white paper published by SiriusDecisions, titled "Sales 2.0: Don't Believe the Hype," predicted that collaboration will increase in importance for sales organizations: "Traditionally, long-tenured salespeople have been able to leverage their relationships to access and secure the resources they need; in a 2.0 world, ad hoc sales teams will form based on unique opportunities spanning business units and product sets as complex customer requirements evolve. In all cases, the various roles must be able to communicate and share information." In other words, you need to be on your best behavior when partnering.

Today, you can assemble a killer team within minutes of qualifying a high-potential opportunity:

> ➤ You send an instant message to your technical systems engineer to confirm whether or not the prospect's environment is conducive for the solution.

> ➤ Once you get a green light, you chat online with a channel manager to inquire about the type of coverage you have in that prospect's area for support, or glance at the technical support site to see if anyone

from the prospect's organization has downloaded a free evaluation of the solution.

> Next, you check your field partner's Outlook calendar to see if he or she is planning a visit in the prospect's location—and then you can invite the district manager to come along.

> You e-mail the marketing coordinator to ask him or her to schedule an executive briefing, and task them to build in some co-op advertising dollars or to write a glossy case study on the prospect.

> You send an e-mail to your financial analyst to crunch some numbers and calculate a strong return on investment that the prospect can expect in the first twelve months after purchase; and you have the customer support rep send out a demo of the solution for six weeks prior to commitment.

> Finally, you contact the legal department and ask them to review the terms in the proposal that the sales coordinator will draft up. Guess who's running with this sale? Touchdown! The inside sales rep makes it happen.

SECRETS OF STRUCTURING A GOOD INSIDE AND FIELD PARTNERSHIP

If you are trying to get a handle on your personal relationships, you might start with psychology (your parents' expectations; where you fell in the birth order of your siblings) or fortune-telling (examining how the stars were aligned when you were born). In order to get a handle on your sales partnerships, you need to look at how your organization structures its sales teams, because that structure is going to be at the root of everything you think is wrong—or right—with your field partnerships.

If you are like most inside sales reps, you are probably working within the traditional sales structure: inside supports the field, and you have to partner with one, or even several, field reps. Some of these forced partnerships are successful, and some are not. The successful ones collaborate well and bring in more revenue; the unsuccessful ones spend too much time in conflict, which usually hurts sales. Who's to blame?

It may be that your organization has inadvertently set your team up to fail from the get-go.

How Inside Organizations May Be Set Up to Fail

Setting up an inside sales organization isn't easy. Unfortunately, and inadvertently, many well-intentioned high-level executives tend to set up inside sales organizations to fail. Often, personality conflicts between field and sales reps are actually rooted in problems with the structure of the partnership itself. Such problems include the following.

Inside Headcount Is Too Low. Numbers talk. When organizations build their inside sales force, they may not hire enough people. When the few reps hired are assigned to work with many field partners, this can impact how they work as a team—the inside partner is spread too thin, and the field partners get frustrated. Sales organizations must make a stand and build up their inside teams in proportion to the field.

The Ratio of Field to Inside Reps Is Too High. Low head count in inside versus field reps may impact the ratios of one to the other when teams are put together. The ideal ratio is 1:1. But if the ratio of field to inside reps is too high (I've seen it as high as 9:1), communication may suffer.

Lack of Respect from the Field. If the organization sees its inside reps as second-class citizens, then their field reps are set up to mistrust or misunderstand the full potential of the team. They will insist on the inside reps providing half-baked leads or opportunities, or they'll cancel appointments with well-qualified leads because the inside reps found them, or they'll expect the inside reps to help them on brainless administrative tasks they could do themselves.

Long Sales Cycle. Inside sales team members need easy wins to keep them motivated to focus on the daily grind of pounding out calls and e-mails. It's important for the inside reps to have an easy, low-cost solution to provide early adoption opportunities for their prospect. Product evaluations are a good vehicle and can convert to a potential sale. A long sales cycle just makes it harder to see results.

New Messaging = New Confusion. If your product focus changes constantly, it confuses your inside reps and keeps them from positioning the product effectively.

Not Sharing the Same Tools. Field reps like to be out on the road. They've never had much patience with data entry and managing their various online tools. Sales 2.0 tools and technologies open up possibilities for more sharing of critical data and knowledge.

Quota Goals That are Unrealistic and Too Late. Everyone is driven by their quota, and compensation issues are important. Unfortunately, it is too common for sales teams to get their quotas assigned too late and much higher than expected. This puts them behind before they begin, and impacts both their productivity and their focus.

Disconnected Marketing. If your marketing department is off doing their own thing, blasting out to thousands of disqualified leads they never bothered to scrub—and expecting the inside reps to follow up—the reps don't have a chance. When leads are this bad, it inevitably affects the lead conversion process. Unfortunately, marketing gets away clean and the inside reps get blamed for doing a poor job!

Providing Inside Training That Is Field Focused. Skills training is great when it is appropriate to the team receiving it. Unfortunately, inside reps are often trained in field sales skills that have very little to do with their roles. Inside sales requires a very different skill set than field sales, and training that is appropriate to their needs just makes sense.

Too Much Technology. Field salespeople are selective about the technology they use (because most of it must be portable). Inside reps have the opposite problem: too much technology and too many cool tools can paralyze them, or even create ways for them to avoid doing what they have been chartered to do by doing busywork.

Why Can't Everyone Just Get Along? There is a tremendous loss of productivity and morale when field reps and inside teams are at war and fight over every opportunity. This type of dissention affects the teams, managers, department, and the entire organization.

The Best Structure for Effective Field-Inside Teams

In order for the partnership of field and inside teams to work, the external and internal structures must be strong. If you are not getting organizational support for your partnership, you can still try to work proactively with your field partner toward a common good.

Leadership Support. Leadership starts at the top. Your manager must share his or her vision about what they expect from an integrated team-selling approach. This requires a strong manager who does not waste time mediating between two kids crying about who took the toy. Since the inside rep and field rep usually have different managers they report to, both managers must be on the same page.

Reporting Structure. Many organizations have their inside teams reporting to the marketing or operations departments, and their field organization reporting directly to the sales organization. When each member of a specific team is reporting to a different division of the company, needs, expectations, and requirements will conflict—and so will the team members.

Team Roles and Responsibilities. Determine who does what, how you will carve out the partnership, and who will handle which roles and responsibilities. Both partners must understand not only their common purpose (expectations), but the division of labor. Who is accountable for what? Begin by clearly defining what exactly the inside and field team members should be doing. What are the performance indicators? What are the metrics? Be sure to address each of the following areas:

> Geography: city, state, sales territory, and so on
> Regions: East, West, Central, and so forth
> Industry verticals: health care, financial, government, education, and so forth
> Revenue threshold: enterprise, mid-market, small/medium-sized business levels, and so on
> Accounts distribution: named accounts, international accounts, and so on

Each team member must know exactly what he or she is responsible for. Confusion leads to squabbles, and that will break up the team.

Expectations. Your team's expectations must be clear right from the start. The best expectations are that the team will work together toward the common good. Team members must be in constant communication rather than withholding information because each sees the other as a threat. If trust is gone and the team members are working separately, the team suffers and sales suffer as a result.

The Hand-Off Process. Customer engagement rules must also be defined. When will the hand-off happen? If this is not spelled out, inside and field reps will be territorial and compete against each other. The hand-off threshold may be under a certain dollar amount, such as the $15,000 mark, or it may focus on key accounts that stay with the inside sales team. Be careful about limiting the hand-off to being under a certain amount, as this may set it up to shrink the size of the deal.

Compensation. Both teams must have incentives in place to recognize (and reward) overachievement. Commission, MBOs (Managing by Objectives) should be clearly defined to avoid confusion; account owners should be designated in advance.

Complementary Skill Strengths. Field teams utilize different skills than inside teams. The field is more strategic and visionary, the inside is more tactical and reactive. The inside team is excellent at managing information, and the field team is strong at merchandising strategies. It is important to understand the skills each contributes, and to let each play their best game.

Feedback and Continuous Measurement. In sales, things change constantly. This means your team needs to be measured, monitored, and improved when necessary. Regular feedback from each other, and from your manager, will help identify areas requiring further attention. Pay attention!

When these structures are in place, your partnership will have an excellent chance of firing on all cylinders. The more people that see your plan and the more you communicate it, the stronger the commitment will be. Table 10-1 illustrates how partnership roles can be articulated in an agreement.

START STRONG

In Chapter 2, "Introducing," we discussed the importance of the first impression you make on the customer. This also applies to setting the expectations and starting smart with your partner right from the beginning. Honing your skills in the following areas will help you start strong and stay strong.

Communicate

What is the single biggest complaint coming from partnerships that fail? There was no communication. There must be regular, consistent, clear communication between the inside and field teams at all times. Partners must communicate on everything regarding their territory—

Table 10-1. Sample Inside-Field Partner Agreement

Team	General Roles and Responsibilities	Primary Activities
Inside Sales	➤ Involved in the entire sales cycle ➤ Specific responsibilities include lead generation and strategy on target accounts; designing marketing strategies that continue to reinforce branding opportunities ➤ Provides strong, consistent phone and online support and establishes up-sell and cross-selling opportunities ➤ Helps neutralize the need to have a field salesperson go on-site ➤ Manages geographically undesirable accounts ➤ Develops and grows the low-volume business of $50K and under ➤ Manages installed base or "Greenfield" accounts ➤ Aligns closely with field team on target account strategy	
Field Sales	➤ Handles face time with accounts, merchandising, branding strategy; works large accounts at the major trade shows ➤ Manages major business ➤ Manages large independent business ➤ Manages the high-volume business ➤ Helps the low-volume transition ➤ Reviews goals and strategies on target accounts with inside team members	

issues, activities, customers, accounts, numbers, expectations—on a daily, weekly, and monthly basis.

Take the time up front to establish a communication strategy. How often do you want to talk, e-mail, and so forth? The better your communication, the more trust and respect you will develop and the more collaborative you will be.

Take a Work Style Inventory

Determine your individual work styles, and take a brief inventory of your partners to see how well you can work together. Often, a bad partnership will occur, not due to personality problems, but because the work styles are completely different. In the beginning, ask questions such as: *"What is your preference on how to work with an account? What are your strengths? How would you like us to support each other? How can we come together regularly to discuss and review our opportunities? Do you want to know about each lead, or do you want a weekly update?"* The answers you get will help you figure out your styles:

> *Detail oriented.* Likes to have all data and resources researched and analyzed; has difficulty making decisions without this in place

> *Interpersonally oriented.* Likes to motivate people and get them engaged; lacks follow-through with commitments

> *Team oriented.* Likes to work with others and follow their lead; has difficulty with independent work

> *Vision oriented.* Likes to take charge and set the vision for the account; doesn't have a need to work with others, and usually doesn't, unless delegating to them

> *Technically oriented.* Loves the technology and thinks that's what the customer is buying; has little tolerance for individuals who do not grasp technical concepts

Sharing Your Territory Plan

Remember in Chapter 1, Time Management, where you outlined a strategic and tactical territory plan? It's time to revisit that plan and share it with your field partner. This will turn into the most significant discussion the two of you can have.

Setting Agreements

Now put your agreements together. In the beginning, you may want to establish clear expectations and guidelines, so a quick e-mail outlining what you've agreed upon is always a good idea:

> Dear Bob,
>
> I'm looking forward to working together and have outlined the twenty-five accounts in our financial vertical. Please review that I'm on track with these accounts. Each week, I plan on prospecting into these target accounts and building org charts, identifying potential opportunities, up-selling, and so on.
>
> I will keep you in the loop on my progress on a regular basis and I expect to also be updated on any communications you engage in with these accounts.
>
> I look forward to generating revenue together as a team!

Are You Ready to Partner?

In my trainings, I can expect to hear at least forty-five minutes of complaining from inside reps about their field partners. Few, however, seem to consider that the problem may be closer to home!

Are you ready to partner? What qualities do you bring to a partnership? What are your selling attributes? Are you a good partner? What makes people want to work with you (or not)? What is your level of commitment, compromise, and communication? Are you worthy of partnering? Do you trust yourself enough to trust working with others? What is it about you that encourages people to put you in the driver's seat? How hard are you on yourself? How can you spend less time in judgment about others and more time creating partnerships?

Below are the four most important qualities people expect from a good partner. Take this opportunity to audit yourself to see if you are partnership worthy. You may need to change your work style, or your approach to partnering. Instead of your old, go-it-alone habits, you may need to adopt synergistic, cooperative, and—yes!—fun business strategies.

1. Your Reputation and Skills

You have a well-earned reputation for succeeding, are trustworthy in your business dealings, and have a sense of what a win-win relationship looks and feels like. You are visible within your team, department, and company, and have a strong positive reputation.

Audit Yourself. Be honest about how others see you. If you don't know, ask a trusted colleague in the organization to give you feedback.

2. Your Communication

You communicate effectively with others—verbally, in writing, and through e-mail. You are a good listener and know what to look for in an opportunity. You are quick to respond, have strong follow-through, and know how to set realistic expectations.

Audit Yourself. If your communication skills need work, then do your homework! This book outlines many ways to improve your communication, both on the phone and online. If you need more help, get a coach or take a course.

3. Your Initiative

You are ready to think outside of the box because you are flexible and open to new ideas. You take the initiative to help on new projects, which may provide you with increased visibility.

Audit yourself. It can be hard to take initiative if you are used to reacting all the time, but give it a try. I guarantee you will like the feeling!

4. Your Attributes

You bring valuable skills—the very ones we have been discussing throughout this book—to the table.

Audit Yourself. Start adding up your list of attributes you bring that would be of value when forming your new partnership. For example:

> Knowledge of SFDC
> Online sleuth—knows precall research well
> Resourceful
> Quick follow-through

> ➤ Excellent communicator
> ➤ Strong interpersonal skills
> ➤ Ability to simplify complex issues
> ➤ Hard-working and diligent
> ➤ Detail-oriented
> ➤ Has technical strength
> ➤ Understands and can articulate the company vision
> ➤ Deep penetration into key accounts
> ➤ Strong business tracking
> ➤ Strengthens relationships with partners

CREATING STRATEGIC ALLIANCES AND PARTNERSHIPS

The inside-field partnership is designed to support and maximize penetration into a particular territory. As such, it is definitive and tangible. But there is another type of partnership that requires more creativity on your part to make it successful: a strategic alliance or partnership with another company. Such powerful collaborations can catapult you and your company into a new era of growth in your life, career, and business.

A strategic alliance is one in which the whole is greater than the sum of its parts. You build relationships that enable you to reach new high-potential prospects, clients, and customers, often with a more complete and valuable product or service offering. For example, your strategic alliance with a rep for a hardware manufacturer may pay off when she recommends your software solution to her newest customer.

Alliances help you see the big picture, and they will outlive your partnership with your field partner. Your strategic alliances will help you understand yourself and your solution in different ways, and will ultimately open you up to a new market and target audience for your solution. Classic strategic alliances you may know include Disney movie characters given away with a Happy Meal at McDonald's, or a Starbucks located inside a Barnes & Noble bookstore.

The Components of a Good Alliance or Partnership

According to Judy Feld and Ernest Oriente, authors of *SmartMatch Alliances,* fun partnerships and strong alliances have the following components:

- ➤ *Win-win:* each alliance partner benefits and thrives in the partnership
- ➤ *Low- to no-risk:* you don't spend money unless you make money
- ➤ *Easy to develop:* the easier it is to create the alliance, the better it will be in the long term
- ➤ *High leverage:* you must invest some time and effort in keeping the alliance strong
- ➤ *Low- to no-cost:* you brainstorm together, and substitute creative thinking for big money
- ➤ *Flexible:* solid alliances are easy-in, easy-out, and easy-to-revise as needs arise
- ➤ *Just-in-time:* your alliance is there when you call on it, ready to go

Finding High-Potential Alliance Partners

Where do you begin to find a match? To start, you need to get away from your old patterns of thinking.

- ➤ Move away from a "go-it-alone" mentality and look to collaborate with others
- ➤ Move away from one-dimensional ideas and toward a matrix of ideas
- ➤ Move away from in-person and move toward virtual
- ➤ Move away from local and move toward global
- ➤ Move away from risk averse and look at creating abundance.

You don't want to turn to your competitors as potential partners. Remember, you need to think big picture. Instead, look at a noncompeting company that sells to the same individuals and/or businesses you're targeting, or think of a product or solution that gets implemented before or after your solution (e.g., hardware for your software).

If you're having trouble coming up with companies to partner with, carefully examine your target audience, because these clues will lead you to finding a complementary solution. Ask yourself some of the following questions:

> Where do the customers of your prime potential partners live, shop, and work?
> What publications does your target audience read?
> What professional trade organizations do they belong to?
> What radio shows do they tune in to?
> What social networking sites do they subscribe to?
> Why do your prospects need your product or solution?

Then, do what you do best. Start calling and networking to create new partnerships!

Become Part of the Conversation

Perhaps you just learned you are connected to someone through a mutual friend, or that your prospect has just left his or her company after seven years. Or perhaps you have just participated in an online discussion about users who have questions about an area in which you have expertise. Social networking is alive and kicking—and it's not going away. In fact, more outlets are being created all the time.

If done responsibly and professionally, social networking can generate additional opportunities. It can help you find new clients and alliances, build up a buzz about your product, open you up to the job market, get feedback when researching, and so much more. Just remember to pay attention to the "five Be's":

1. *Become part of the conversation.* The days of single contacts are gone; social networking rules require that you engage in relevant discussions.

2. *Be trustworthy.* The social networking landscape is all about building a "trust" network of friends and colleagues who act as trusted advisors for you.

3. *Be responsible.* Don't just blanket your entire business base of contacts, asking them to be your friends, share Tweets, and link up with you. It is better to have a powerful online presence than to just scratch the surface. Become knowledgeable and align with your target audience's social networking habits.

4. *Be creative.* If you are only targeting people in your space, everyone starts looking the same. The key to networking is to be open to trying new paths.

5. *Be alert.* Take time to understand everyone's hot buttons. Helping them can help you. When you speak with someone, and realize you have a contact for them, match them up! Many times you can get what you want later by helping others get what they want now.

6. *Be casual.* Networking allows you to be yourself and not work with any canned scripts. Any formality will just distance your prospects. Your authentic self is so much more attractive—but don't be *too* authentic (no drunken pictures at the office party!).

7. *Be generous.* The successful social networkers are generous with their knowledge and like to share content with others. Whether you upload a slide presentation, put a white paper, or write an e-book, these are ways to be generous in your efforts to partner. Give information in order to get information.

Cubicle Chronicles

──────────────── **Reality Check** ────────────────

Here are some typical scenarios between inside sales and field partners. I know they're typical because I hear these problems *all the time.* If any of these sound familiar, and you know you are not in the wrong, review the scenario and get ready to push back!

Cheating Charlie: You discover that your field partner, Charlie, has negotiated a contract you were working on at an unbelievably low price. He bundled it in with his opportunity, and wants to run his order through his forecast and enter it into the sales system and ultimately get credit on it.

Reality Check: Something smells fishy here. Have a heart-to-heart with Charlie. Let him know you are not comfortable about this and don't want to have your name attached to this deal. Then tell your manager about your discussion. Make sure you cover yourself, because you may be the first to blame if exposed.

Mistrusting Melinda: After spending weeks waiting for Melinda to provide you with your key target accounts and strategies, she has taken 80 percent of the list and declared it "off-limits"!

Reality Check: Melinda is sending a clear signal that she doesn't trust you yet—you must prove your worth. Don't take it personally. She may have been burned by inside sales reps in the past. Instead of fighting her, take the 20 percent of the accounts she gave you and sell the hell out of them! Once she sees what you are capable of, she'll relinquish control.

Delegating David: David strikes again. He has dumped about four major projects, RFPs, and customer reference projects on your lap—just like last month. Of course, he has invited you to several high-level demos, and is very excited about some new business opportunities in your joint territory.

Reality Check: It's a compliment to feel wanted and needed, but you must push back and ask David what his priorities are. This type of personality has a way of engulfing you in his stuff, and it doesn't stop there. Set up boundaries for yourself and for David.

Crisis Chris: Chris has the habit of calling you on his way to the airport with frantic requests to look up information for him. He wants everything done yesterday, and he usually gets it because he is so frantic, emotional, persuasive—and politically aligned at the highest levels.

Reality Check: We discussed this sort of problem way back in Chapter 1. Just because David approaches *his* business reactively doesn't mean you have to. Instead of being his slave, help Chris organize, prioritize, and work more proactively by pushing back: Ask more questions to get a better understanding of the real urgency of his requests. At least every other time it's probably something that can wait.

Invisible Ivan: You find out that Ivan just stood up at the last regional sales meeting and said that he cannot understand exactly what value the inside sales organization brings him in terms of leads. Meanwhile, you have sent him countless e-mails and voice mails requesting callbacks, but he has never responded.

Reality Check: Ivan is one of the toughest kinds of reps to support because they never take responsibility—they want to do it all themselves and blame you at the same time! Document and copy your manager on all of your efforts so that others can plainly see that you have been holding up your end. You may also push back here: Ask Ivan to be more specific and to provide you with examples of your wrongdoing.

PARTNERING STRATEGIES

1. Don't let a bad partnership get you down. Be proactive: you can drive the deal.

2. Technology and tools have increased opportunities to partner with more people instantly. Take advantage of them to create strategic alliances and social networking opportunities.

3. Don't be so quick to blame your field partner when things go wrong. It may be that you are both working within a structure that sets you up to fail.

4. You may need to educate your field partner on the value you bring in order to create a more collaborative, trusting, and respectful working partnership. One way to do this is to show that you can get results.

5. Any time you are assigned a new field partner, start strong by

setting expectations and pumping up your level of communication.

6. A partnering plan is essential; it's the most common language you share with your field partner. Build one together and review it regularly.

7. If your partner's poor opinion of you is making you get down on yourself, remember this: You are worth *so much more* than you are giving yourself credit for. Take some time to write down the positive attributes and contributions you can bring to a deal.

8. You never know how a strategic partnership may be formed. Stay alert, read, talk with people . . . you never know when a potential match may come along.

9. Don't let social networking fatigue set in. Build and maintain your qualified contacts.

10. Learn to spend less time judging others and creating partnership problems. Instead, be creative with the partnership you have and remember that two partners who work well together can actually make the job easier.

EPILOGUE

Great work! Take a moment to congratulate yourself: you now know more about inside sales than most salespeople—and their managers—learn in a lifetime. Now what?

Have fun, reward yourself with a mocha or a latte, and put those skills to work! With the sheer volume of e-mails and calls you make each day, *excelling at even one skill will produce exponential results.* I've seen it happen again and again.

Visualize your name at the top of that whiteboard, inhale confidence in yourself and your product or service, know that you have the tools to get the job done—and keep this book handy for quick reference.

Now go out there and kill your numbers!

INDEX